Literacy by Design™

Sourcebook
Volume 2

Program Authors

Linda Hoyt

Michael Opitz

Robert Marzano

Sharon Hill

Yvonne Freeman

David Freeman

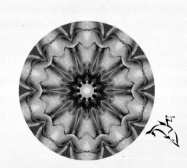

HOUGHTON MIFFLIN HARCOURT

Welcome to Literacy by Design,
Where Reading Is...

Imagining

Thinking

Literacy by Design: Sourcebook Volume 2
Grade 4

Copyright © 2013 by HMH Supplemental
Publishers Inc.

Printed in U.S.A.

ISBN   978-0-547-73457-6

1 2 3 4 5 6 7 8 9 10 0918 21 20 19 18 17 16 15 14 13 12
4500338277   A B C D E F G

Discovering

Questioning

Exploring

UNIT The Early Americas

iv

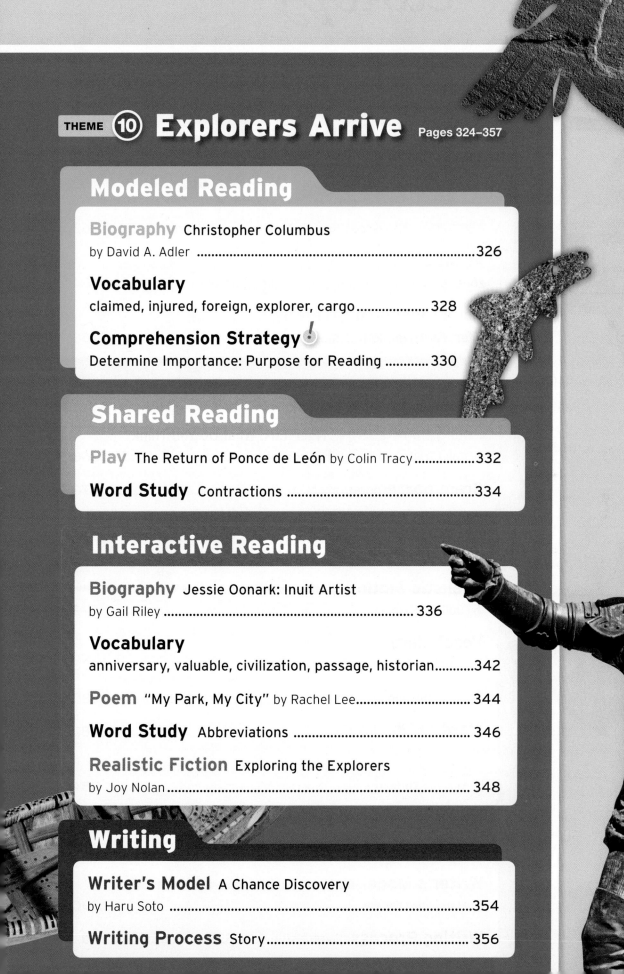

THEME 10 **Explorers Arrive** Pages 324–357

UNIT Under the *Canopy*

THEME (12) Affecting the Rain Forest
Pages 394–427

Modeled Reading

Shared Reading

Interactive Reading

Writing

UNIT Buyers and Sellers

THEME ⑭ Buying Smart

Pages 464–497

UNIT WRITTEN IN STONE

THEME (16) Wearing Away Pages 534–567

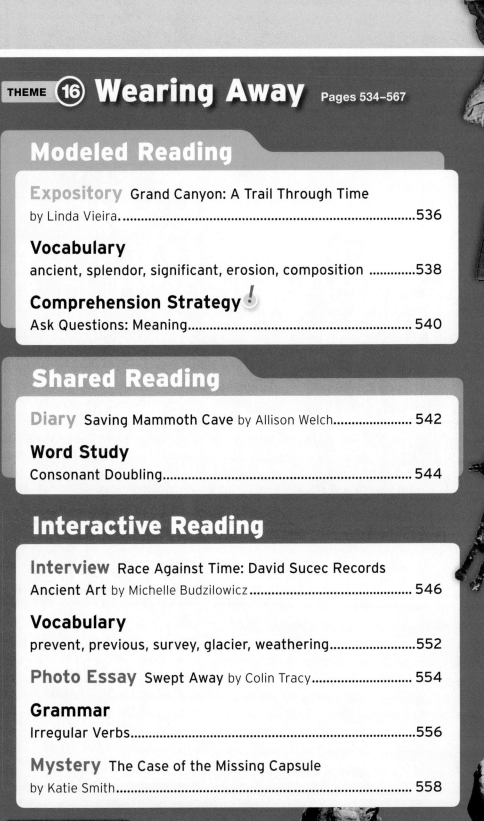

Untitled, circa 1940

An illustration of Jacques Cartier and Native Americans, 1535

C. W. Jefferys (1869–1951)

Viewing

The artist who created this illustration was C. W. Jefferys. He illustrated this scene several hundred years after the event occurred.

1. What is the event pictured? What makes you think so?

2. How do you think the artist's cultural views influenced the way he portrayed the Native people?

3. What do you think the explorers are thinking about as they meet these people? Why do you think that?

4. What changes do you think the artist would have made if he had been with the explorers as they met the Native people?

In This UNIT

In this unit you will read about the Native people of the Americas, explorers, and Native Americans of today.

Native People of North America

Contents

Modeled Reading

Shared Reading

Interactive Reading

Writing

Eagle Boy
A Pacific Northwest Native Tale

Retold by Richard Lee Vaughan   Illustrated by Lee Christiansen

Precise Listening

Precise listening means listening for details in the story. Listen to the focus questions your teacher will read to you.

The Eagle

Symbol of Honor

The Native Americans of Pacific **coastal** areas honor the bald eagle in many ways. This mighty hunter represents power, wisdom, and freedom. The eagle is celebrated in their traditions and art.

Fancy Feathers

Feathers are worn by Pacific Northwest peoples during rituals, dances, and other social events. The feathers symbolize peace, friendship, and good luck.

Did You Know?

In 1782, the United States adopted the bald eagle as its national bird. The federal government monitors the bald eagle **population** to ensure that it remains **plentiful** and healthy. Eagles have been a protected species since 1940, when bald eagles were becoming **scarce**.

Fun Fact!

Eagles have amazing eyesight. A bald eagle can locate a fish from as far as one mile above a **waterway**. It can dive into the water at more than 100 miles an hour, grab the fish with its strong talons, and soar high up into the sky with its prize.

Structured Vocabulary Discussion

When your teacher says a vocabulary word, write all the words that the vocabulary word makes you think of. When your teacher says, "Stop," share your words with a partner. Take turns explaining to each other why you chose the words on your list.

> Throughout the week, add to your vocabulary journal entries. Record new insights and other words that relate to this week's vocabulary.

Picture It

Draw a chart like this in your vocabulary journal. Fill in the boxes with things you might find in a **coastal** area.

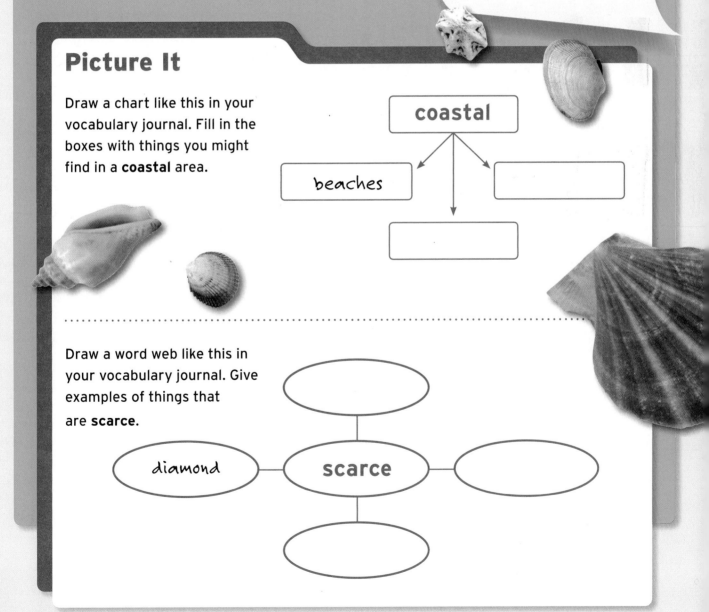

Draw a word web like this in your vocabulary journal. Give examples of things that are **scarce**.

Make Connections
Text to Text, Self, and World

Making connections as you read can help you better understand what you are reading. You can make connections between a selection and other books you have read. You can also make connections between a selection and your own experiences, or things you know about in the world.

A CONNECTION is a link between two ideas.

To make connections, relate your reading to your own life and to the things you have read, heard, and seen.

TURN AND TALK Listen as your teacher reads the following lines from *Eagle Boy*. With a partner, discuss connections you can make between *Eagle Boy* and your own experiences.

• Think about how Eagle Boy feels. Have you ever had similar feelings?

• Can you think of a character in a movie who reminds you of *Eagle Boy*? In what way?

Eagle Boy turned toward the flames. "Let them go hungry!" he shouted in anger. "Just as they left me to do."

In silence, the Great Eagle watched the boy.

Staring into the fire, Eagle Boy remembered the canoes paddling away. He remembered Kwish-kwish-ee laughing at him. But he also remembered Chuh-coo-duh-bee slipping him food. And the eagles bringing him fish and saving his life.

TAKE IT WITH YOU Making connections helps you compare new ideas to things you already know. Read the chart below to see how one student made connections to *Eagle Boy*.

In the Text	This Reminds Me Of...	Text, Self, or World?
Eagle Boy is trying to decide whether to help his people. He is angry with them, but he remembers how others have helped him when he needed it.	 I know that Native Americans helped the Pilgrims. The Pilgrims were having trouble surviving in their new land.	✔ text ○ self ○ world
Eagle Boy shouts at Great Eagle because he is so angry at his people.	 Sometimes I fight with my brother. We shout at each other. If he asks for help with his homework later, I don't want to help him at first.	○ text ✔ self ○ world
Eagle Boy thinks about how the eagles and his friend bring him food.	People around our country come together to help other people during a crisis, such as a hurricane.	○ text ○ self ✔ world

Sequoyah

Developed the Cherokee Alphabet

Born
1776, near Tuskeegee, Tennessee

Died
1843, near Tyler, Texas

by Chris Parker

Have you heard of the giant redwood trees known as sequoias? These huge trees are named after a great Cherokee leader, Sequoyah.

Sequoyah was born around 1776 in the Smoky Mountains of Tennessee. Information about his childhood is practically nonexistent. As a young man he worked as a farmer, blacksmith, and silversmith. In the War of 1812, along with many other Cherokees, he fought on the side of the United States.

In his contacts with settlers and soldiers, Sequoyah saw the importance of written words. Written messages could be carried across long distances without changing their meanings. Written records could be kept for years without being forgotten. The Cherokees did not have a written language. They could only speak their language.

To preserve his people's history, Sequoyah decided to create a Cherokee writing system. He listened carefully to the sounds of the Cherokee language.

He created different symbols for each sound. After years of work, his system was ready. It was made up of 85 symbols. Each symbol stood for a syllable. The symbols could be rearranged to write down any spoken Cherokee word.

Sequoyah's written system turned out to be very easy to learn. His first student was his daughter, Ayoka. In 1821, the two of them gave public demonstrations. They would stand far apart, write down messages to each other, and read them to a crowd.

Cherokee alphabet created by Sequoyah

The Cherokee realized how useful the writing system would be. Thousands of Cherokee people learned to read and write. Books were translated into Cherokee. A newspaper, *The Cherokee Phoenix*, was established in 1828. Now Cherokees could send letters, keep business records, and record their history.

Sequoyah is considered the first person in history to invent a written language alone. In honor of his incredible, towering achievement, he was awarded a silver medal, and the world's largest tree—the giant redwood known as sequoia—is named after him. ■

Time Line

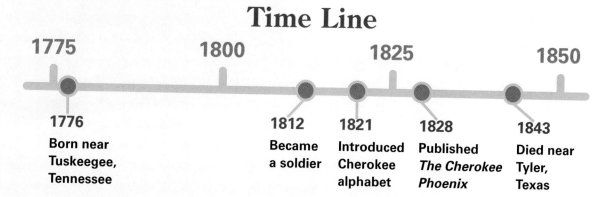

| 1775 | 1800 | 1825 | 1850 |

1776
Born near Tuskeegee, Tennessee

1812
Became a soldier

1821
Introduced Cherokee alphabet

1828
Published *The Cherokee Phoenix*

1843
Died near Tyler, Texas

Atian Meets Crazy Horse

June 29

South Dakota, USA

After driving nonstop with my family for four days, I finally saw the Crazy Horse Memorial in the Black Hills of South Dakota.

I just stared at it in disbelief. It's huge! It's indestructible. It's being carved out of a mountain. Right now, you only see Crazy Horse's face. But when it's finished, you'll see him sitting on his horse and looking across the land. It will take years to finish the work, but no one is discouraged.

Crazy Horse was an incredible Lakota leader who died more than 100 years ago. He fought to protect the Lakota way of life.

Looking at the monument made me think about my great-great-great-grandmother. She was a member of the Lakota nation. I wish she could see this awesome memorial.

Atian

CRAZY HORSE—SOUTH DAKOTA

Prefixes *non-*, *in-* and *dis-*

Activity One

About Prefixes

A *prefix* is a word part added to the beginning of a word. Knowing the meaning of a prefix can help you understand the meaning of a new word. For example, the prefix *non-* means "not," "without," or "opposite." As your teacher reads Atian's diary entry, listen for words containing the prefixes *non-*, *in-*, and *dis-*.

Prefixes in Context

With a small group, reread Atian's diary and make a list of words with the prefixes *non-*, *in-*, and *dis-*. In a chart like the one below, write each prefix, root word, the whole word, and its meaning.

PREFIX	ROOT WORD	WORD	MEANING
non	stop	nonstop	without stopping, no stopping

Activity Two

Explore Words Together

Work with a partner to write down the meaning of each word on the right. Then add the prefix *non-*, *in-*, or *dis-* to each word to make new words. With your partner, write down the meaning of each new word. Talk with your partner about how the prefix changes the meaning of each word.

fiction   direct
trust   honest
ability

Activity Three

Explore Words in Writing

Write a diary entry about an amazing event in your life. Use words with the prefixes *non-*, *in-*, or *dis-*. Then share your diary entry with a partner. Have your partner find and circle the words with the prefixes.

South Dakota

Crazy Horse Memorial
★

How the Crow Got its Color

A TRADITIONAL LAKOTA TALE

retold by Molly Smith

Long ago, the crows of Crow Nation were as white as snow. These snow-white crows were known for their nosy and noisy ways. The crows were faithful friends of the buffalo, the great *ta-tan-ka,* of Buffalo Nation. When the buffalo were in danger, the crows sounded warning cries. They would even perch on the horns of a buffalo and speak right into its ear.

The largest and loudest crow was the crow leader. His calls could be heard across the prairie for miles. The buffalo knew the big, white crow and listened to his warnings.

The Lakota people lived on the prairies and depended on the region's buffalo for survival. They were respectful of their animal neighbors and never hunted more than they needed. They used every part of the buffalo—the meat for food and the hide for making clothes and homes.

How are the Lakota like the people in Eagle Boy's village?

In those times, the Lakota hunted the great buffalo on foot, which was very difficult and dangerous work. They often moved their villages from one place to another as they traveled for miles in search of a herd. When a herd was spotted, the Lakota braves spent much time planning and preparing how to capture the powerful *ta-tan-ka.*

The crows made things difficult for the hunters. Soaring high above the plains, they circled the skies looking for news to report. Sometimes they flew in flocks that looked like white clouds against the blue skies.

One day when they spied the Lakota hunters approaching a herd, the crows swooped down to warn the buffalo and speak.

"Caw, caw, caw! *Ta-tan-ka*, our big, hairy cousins, listen to our warning. Hunters are near. We have seen fifty men with stone-tipped weapons, which they will use against you."

Have you ever felt the way the hunters must feel? When?

When the buffalo heard the warnings, they flew across the plains to escape the hunters, sending giant clouds of brown dust flying at their feet. The great stampede shook the ground like an earthquake. The buffalo were fast and covered great distances in a short time. It might take the Lakota days, weeks, or even months to find the herd again. When the hunters returned to the circle of tipis empty-handed, the people felt defeated and discouraged.

Two-Word Technique

Write down two words that reflect your thoughts about each page. Discuss them with your partner.

"Once again, Crow Nation has warned the buffalo," the hunters reported. "We must act to stop this nonsense."

The hungry and tired people gathered in council to decide what to do about their desperate situation. An elder among them spoke.

"We must capture the big, white crow," he said. "Then we must teach him our ways. We respect the birds that fly above us, but we must survive. The crows must discontinue warning the buffalo or we will go hungry."

The elder called for a large buffalo skin, one with the head and horns still attached. He placed the skin over the back of his nephew, a young hunter.

"Here is my plan," he said to his people. "When we find the buffalo again, my nephew will join the herd in disguise and graze with it. Our people will then prepare to hunt the buffalo. When the large, white crow arrives to ruin our hunt, my nephew will capture him and bring him back to our council."

Have you ever had to tell someone to stop doing something? What was it?

And so the people accepted the plan and prepared for yet another journey. As soon as they found the herd of buffalo, the people set their plan in motion.

The women sewed the buffalo skin together and placed it on the young hunter's body. They used needles made from buffalo bones and thread made from buffalo hair. They even sprinkled the hunter with buffalo oil to make him smell like a member of Buffalo Nation. When the young man was ready, they sent him to the herd.

The young brave crept up slowly behind the herd. He pretended to graze on the tall grasses of the prairie. The big, shaggy beasts snorted contentedly, feeding in the sun. They did not notice the newcomer.

Have you ever seen a movie in which a character used a disguise to trick somebody? What happened?

The hunters crept silently from their camp, bows strung and ready for the hunt. Once they neared the herd, the crows swooped down to the herd with loud caws. The big, white crow was the first to arrive.

"Caw, caw, caw! Listen to me, my large, hairy cousins! The hunters are approaching from the ravine. Run! Beware of their arrows!"

At once, the mighty buffalo stampeded with a great force that shook the ground. Only the young hunter remained quiet under his shaggy buffalo skin. He pretended to go on grazing as before. So the big, white crow perched on his shoulders.

"Caw, caw, caw! My cousin, can you not hear my warning? Save yourself! Run! Catch your brothers and sisters!"

Suddenly, the young man reached out from under the buffalo skin and grabbed the crow. With a rawhide string, he tied the big bird's feet together and fastened them to a stone. No matter how the big, white crow struggled, he could not escape.

The young man brought the leader of Crow Nation to the circle of tipis, and the people gathered in council. The elder spoke.

"You have caused us to know hunger many times," he said. "Our people worry because their bellies remain empty. We do not wish to hurt the buffalo—only to survive."

At this moment, an angry hunter stood up.

"This will teach you," he cried. And before anyone could stop him, he yanked the crow from the hands of the elder and thrust him into the coals in the middle of the council.

Luckily, the string that held the stone burned through almost at once and the crow flew out of the coals, but not before the embers charred his feathers. He was no longer white, but black.

"Caw, caw, caw!" he cried, flying away. "I take pity on the Lakota people. I will stop warning the buffalo, and so will all the crows of Crow Nation. I promise! Caw, caw, caw!"

And so the crow escaped. But ever since, crows have had black feathers to remind them that the Lakota people need the buffalo to survive.

Does this story remind you of any other stories you know? How?

306

Think and Respond

Reflect and Write

- You and your partner each wrote two words about every page in the selection as you read. Discuss these words and choose two that you feel best reflect the story.

- On one side of an index card, write down the two words you chose. On the other, write down connections you and your partner make to these words. Remember that these connections can be to other texts, your life, or things you know.

Prefixes in Context

Search through *How the Crow Got Its Color* to find words that begin with *non-*, *in-*, and *dis-*. Tell what each word means without the prefix. Then use what you know about the prefix to help you define the whole word.

Turn and Talk

MAKE CONNECTIONS: TEXT TO TEXT, SELF, AND WORLD

Discuss with a partner what you have learned so far about making connections to things you have read, heard, or seen before.

- What does it mean to make connections when you read?

- How does making connections help you in your reading?

Think about one connection you've made with *How the Crow Got Its Color*. Talk about your connection with a partner. Be sure to use details to explain your thinking.

Critical Thinking

With a group, brainstorm a list of things you need to survive and write them on the left side on a piece of paper. On the right side of the piece of paper, write down the ways that the Lakota used the buffalo. Discuss these questions together.

- How many elements of the Lakotas' needs did the buffalo provide? Why is the buffalo important to the Lakota people?

- What would have happened to the Lakota people if the crow had not cooperated?

Vocabulary

Living Off the Land

PEOPLE OF THE PACIFIC NORTHWEST

Native Americans of the Northwest coast, such as the Skagit, lived near the Pacific Ocean. The ocean and rivers supplied seafood and fish. **Surplus** salmon caught in the summer would be dried and eaten during the winter.

PEOPLE OF THE PLAINS

Many Native American groups lived on a flat, grassy **plain**. Plains people were nomadic, moving their villages from place to place following the roaming herds of buffalo. The buffalo was a source of food, clothing, shelter, and tools.

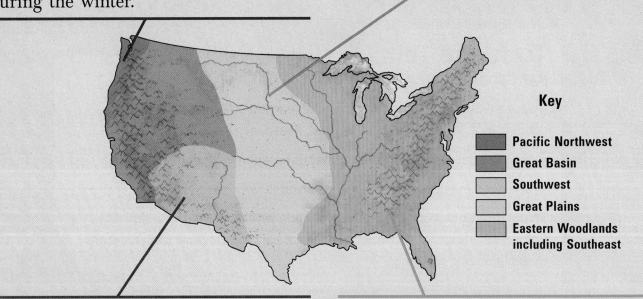

Key

- Pacific Northwest
- Great Basin
- Southwest
- Great Plains
- Eastern Woodlands including Southeast

PEOPLE OF THE SOUTHWEST

Some Native Americans of the Southwest were farmers. Water is a valuable **resource** in this region for **survival**. The Pueblo people would hold festivals and ceremonies to bring rain for their crops: corn, squash, and beans.

PEOPLE OF THE SOUTHEAST

Large amounts of rain produce rich **vegetation** in the Southeast. Some Native American groups, such as the Seminole, used herbs as medicine. Today, many people use some of these same herbs to treat pain and illness.

plain   survival   surplus   vegetation   resource

Structured Vocabulary Discussion

Review the vocabulary words above. Group the words into two categories:

• Words that describe things in nature.

• Words that describe something that happens.

When your teacher calls on you, be ready to explain why each word belongs in its category.

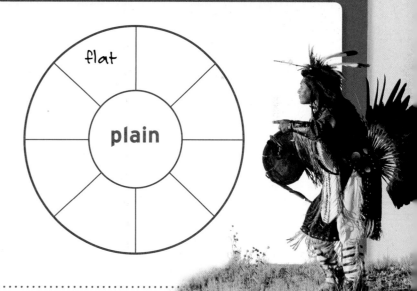

Throughout the week, add to your vocabulary journal entries. Record new insights and other words that relate to this week's vocabulary.

Picture It

Draw charts like these in your vocabulary journal. Fill in the empty spaces with words that describe the appearance and climate of a **plain**.

flat

plain

Fill in each box of the chart with a **resource** you use every day and can't live without.

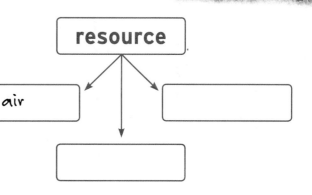

resource

air

MORNING LIGHT

translated from a traditional Papago chant

Downy white feathers
Are moving beneath
The sunrise
And along the edge of the world.

The morning star is up.
I cross the mountains
Into the light of the sea.
A white mountain is far to the west.
It stands beautiful.
It has brilliant white arches of light—
A surplus of light from its height—
Bending down towards the earth.

Pueblo Oven Bread

Native people of the Southwest have been baking bread for thousands of years in outdoor ovens, which Spanish settlers called *hornos*. To recapture a taste of Pueblo history, ask an adult to help you bake the same bread in your oven at home!

INGREDIENTS

1 package of yeast

¼ cup of warm water

¼ cup honey

½ tablespoon shortening

½ teaspoon salt

1 cup of hot water

5 cups flour

DIRECTIONS

1. Preheat the oven to 350 degrees. Prearrange your ingredients.

2. Dissolve the yeast in ¼ cup warm water. Set aside.

3. Combine shortening, honey, and salt in a large bowl. Add 1 cup hot water. Stir the mixture each time you add another ingredient. Let the mixture cool to room temperature.

4. Stir the yeast mixture into the ingredients in the bowl.

5. Add 4 cups flour slowly as you stir to make dough.

6. Knead, punch, press, and squeeze the dough until it's smooth. Do this on a breadboard sprinkled with the last cup of flour.

7. Put the dough into a bowl and cover with a clean cloth. Set it in a warm place until the dough doubles in size. The yeast causes the dough to grow.

8. Repeat step 6. Then shape the dough into two loaves.

9. Place the loaves on a greased cookie sheet. Bake about 1 hour or until lightly browned.

Pueblo oven bread tastes best warm. You can reheat the bread by placing it on the middle rack of your oven with a shallow pan of water underneath.

Prefixes *re-* and *pre-*

Activity One

About Prefixes

Prefixes are used to give a new meaning to a word. By adding a prefix, you can make a word mean something different. For example, the prefix *re-* means "again" or "back" and *pre-* means "before." As your teacher reads the recipe for Pueblo oven bread, listen for words containing the prefixes *re-* and *pre-*.

Prefixes in Context

Share the *re-* and *pre-* words that you heard with a partner. Work together to make a list of words. Read the recipe again and look for more words with *re-* and *pre-*. How many were you able to find altogether?

Activity Two

Explore Words Together

pay	view
new	write
appear	judge

Look at the words on the right with a partner. Work together to make new words using each prefix. Which words work with both *re-* and *pre-*? Make a list of the words that can have either prefix.

Activity Three

Explore Words in Writing

With a partner, choose one word in the activity above that can use both *re-* and *pre-*. Write a sentence using that word with one of the prefixes while your partner writes a sentence using the same word with the other prefix. Then share your sentences. Discuss how the prefix changes the meaning of each sentence.

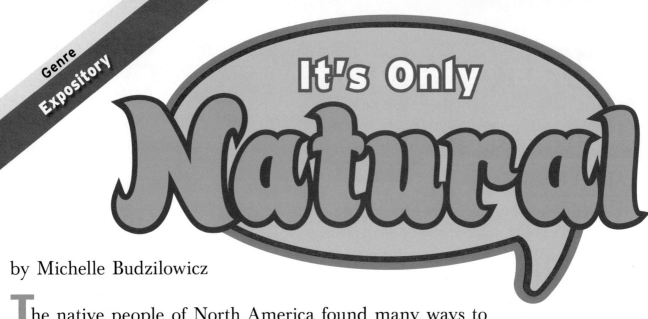

It's Only Natural

by Michelle Budzilowicz

The native people of North America found many ways to meet their basic needs using the resources around them. They also used those resources to invent many useful items. Many people today still use these inventions.

Have you ever used or seen a Native American invention? Let's find out!

Canoes: An Ancient Boat

Canoes and other small boats have been around for a long time. Native Americans who lived on the East coast of North America, like the Algonquin people, developed the boat called the birchbark canoe.

To go through shallow streams, deep lakes, and fast rivers, the Algonquin needed a strong, lightweight vessel. They used the vegetation around them to create their boat. The frame of the canoe was built from cedar trees. They used birch bark to cover the frame. Birch bark is lightweight, smooth, and waterproof. The bark was tied to the boat using tree roots. The outside of the canoe was pretreated with hot resin. Resin is a sticky liquid that becomes hard and waterproof when it dries.

Why is resin rubbed on a canoe?

Canoes Today

The canoe has remained the same shape over the years, but now it is made of other materials, like metal or plastic. People use canoes for outdoor sports. Clubs and organizations even hold canoeing races and long-distance marathons.

Most people use canoes for weekend fun. You can race one down the river or paddle across a calm lake. This boat can do it all!

Why is a canoe well-suited for travel on rivers and lakes?

Partner Jigsaw Technique Read your section with a partner and write down one question. Be prepared to summarize your section and share one question.

Toboggans: Super Sleds

Native Americans living near the Great Lakes made long sleds called toboggans.

These sleds carried heavy loads easily across snow. *Toboggan* comes from the Algonquin word *topaghan*, meaning "a vehicle traveling through snow."

Toboggans were made of two birch boards. Birch is lightweight, which made it good for traveling through the snow. Presoaking the wood in water made it easy to reshape. Giving the front of the sled a 'J' shape let it move quickly over bumps and rocks. The curved pieces of wood were fastened together with moose sinews. Sinew is stringy tissue that holds a muscle to a bone.

How is the toboggan's shape helpful?

Toboggans Today

In modern life, people use toboggans mostly for fun. Some toboggans are long enough that your whole family can sled down a snowy slope together! In 1883, tobogganing was an event in the Winter Olympics. Today it is called the "luge." Athletes in the luge can reach speeds of more than 60 miles per hour!

Snowshoes: A Great Way to Walk

Long ago, Native Americans living in the North invented snowshoes for traveling in deep snow. Snowshoes spread a person's weight over a larger area so that a person doesn't sink into the snow. Early snowshoes were made of young trees that could be bent easily. The webbing of the snowshoe was made from animal hide or sinew. A piece of wood across the middle of the shoe gave support. The Cree people used the longest snowshoes. They were nearly six feet long!

Snowshoes Today

Snowshoeing remains a popular winter activity. Snowshoeing is a favorite event at some winter festivals. One game features runners who jump over hurdles three and a half feet tall. People also like to use snowshoes for winter hiking. Some people even play soccer in snowshoes!

How do snowshoes make people's lives easier?

Lacrosse: America's First Sport

Lacrosse was played in many Native American cultures from the Cherokee to the Iroquois. Players on a team used a long stick to pass a ball back and forth. The ball was carried in a basket on the stick. Many sizes and styles of sticks were crafted from local trees.

Native Americans played the game not only for fun, but also to settle arguments and to test warriors. The Cherokee called the sport "the little brother of war."

Games were played by as many as 1,000 men and sometimes lasted two or three days. The goal areas were marked with rocks or trees and could span from 500 yards to several miles apart. There were no sidelines, so players raced far and wide over the countryside.

Lacrosse Today

Lacrosse is regaining popularity in the United States today. Schools all over the country have lacrosse teams. There are more than 500 college teams in the United States as well as a professional league with teams in ten cities. These exciting games require a great deal of strength and skill.

Native American cultures have passed down many useful items, including some of the tools and games that are now some of our favorite pastimes. Next time you go sledding or paddle a canoe, think about the history behind these inventions!

How is lacrosse similar to other sports today?

Think and Respond

Reflect and Write

- You and your partner have read a section of *It's Only Natural* and written down a question about the section.

- Find partner teams that read other sections of *It's Only Natural*. Ask them to share a summary and a question they asked.

Prefixes *re-* and *pre-* in Context

Look through *It's Only Natural* to find words that begin with *re-* and *pre-*. List each one you find and circle its prefix. Write down how taking off the prefix would change the meaning of the sentence.

Turn and Talk
ASK QUESTIONS

Discuss with a partner what you have learned so far about the strategy of asking questions.

- How does asking questions help you as you read?

- Think about an invention you read about in *It's Only Natural*. What questions do you have about the invention?

Critical Thinking

With a group, choose one of the inventions described in *It's Only Natural*. Brainstorm ways in which Native Americans used the natural environment to create the invention.

Then discuss these questions:

- Did the invention help solve a problem for the Native Americans? How?

- What things might they have observed in the natural world that would have sparked these inventions?

In a biography, an author writes about important events and accomplishments in a real person's life. In this biography, Mariana writes about her grandfather and how he came to the United States from Mexico.

The Path of Education
by Mariana Vasquez

Growing up, my grandfather Ernesto didn't always know what he wanted to be. He knew only that he wanted to learn. This desire would cause him to relocate several times. He moved to new towns and cities every few years to continue his education. My grandfather is inspiring because he never stopped working to get an education. He followed his dreams no matter where they took him.

The writer introduces the real person her biography is about.

Grandfather grew up on a small ranch near Guadalajara, Mexico, called Las Tortugas. *Las Tortugas* means "the turtles" in Spanish. I don't know if my grandfather had any of those on his ranch. But there were cows, pigs, and chickens. Grandfather and his family harvested corn and beans to make a living.

The writer develops the biography with facts and details.

On the ranch, there was only one classroom. Grandfather attended school there until third grade. Then he had a decision to make. He could move and continue his education, or he could stay and work as a rancher. He chose to learn. He moved to a larger town.

In this town, Grandfather attended school until sixth grade. Then, once again, he had to make a decision. He could continue school in a larger town, or he could begin working. Again, he chose to learn. My grandfather continued moving and attending school until he arrived in Guadalajara.

In this big city, Grandfather learned to be an electrician. He also met my grandmother there. In 1983, he moved to the United States and started a family. After years of moving almost nonstop, Grandfather was home.

My grandfather is the smartest, most inspiring person I know. When I am feeling discouraged in school, he tells me that education is indispensable. I couldn't agree more!

> The writer uses transition words and phrases to show the sequence, or order, of events.

> The writer concludes the biography by stating why her grandfather is important.

Respond in Writing

Answer these questions about the biography you just read.

- How does the writer develop the main message of the biography? Use details from the biography to support your answer.

- How does the writer organize events in the biography? Does this order work well? Use details from the biography to explain why or why not.

Writing: Biography

Use the steps of the writing process to create a biography.
The following tips can help make your writing its best.

Prewriting

- Make a list of real people you might like to write about. Then choose one as your subject. The person you choose to write about can be someone you know or a public figure.

- Make a time line of your subject's important moments and accomplishments.

- If the biography is about someone you know, gather information from a primary source, if possible.

- If the biography is about a public figure, use various print, multimedia, and online sources to gather information.

Drafting

- Include your purpose for writing about this person's life.

- Using your time line, write about key events from the person's life in the order that they happened.

- Present information in a way that allows readers to make a meaningful connection with your subject.

- Make sure your biography has a clear beginning, middle, and ending.

Revising

- Check your prewriting to make sure you didn't leave out any details you wanted to include.

- Look for areas of your biography that could use more description or clarification. Use sticky notes to indicate where details and events should be added, if necessary.

- Make sure you use a variety of sentence lengths and beginnings.

Editing

- Check for correct use of verbs in each sentence.

- Make sure you used progressive verb tenses correctly.

- Check that you used singular and plural pronouns correctly.

- Read your writing aloud slowly and quietly to yourself to check for errors.

Publishing

- Choose a creative title for your biography that will hint at what it is about.

- Consider making a poster board of quotes from or about your subject.

- Add captioned photographs of your subject and the places that were important to his or her life story.

- Present your writing to your class and include a short audio or video recording of your subject.

Contents

Explorers Arrive

Christopher Columbus

by David A. Adler

illustrated by John & Alexandra Wallner

Strategic Listening

Strategic listening means listening to understand the selection. Listen to the focus questions your teacher will read to you.

Sailing with Columbus

by Allison Welch

After years of waiting, Columbus left Spain in 1492 for **foreign** lands. The **explorer** and his crew sailed on three ships: the *Nina*, the *Pinta*, and the *Santa Maria*. Columbus had **claimed** that by sailing west on these three ships he could reach the Indies and all the riches it had to offer. Finally the king and queen of Spain had listened to him.

Life at sea was hard for the ninety men in Columbus's crew. The sailors worked long days managing the sails, pumping water out of the ship, and cleaning the decks. Sometimes, even if they were careful, a sailor was **injured**.

The sailors also took care of the **cargo**, which included food, water, and even live animals! The crew had to sleep and cook on the ships' decks. They ate biscuits, pickled or salted meat, dried peas, cheese, and fish. Columbus's sailors were probably happy when these ships finally reached land!

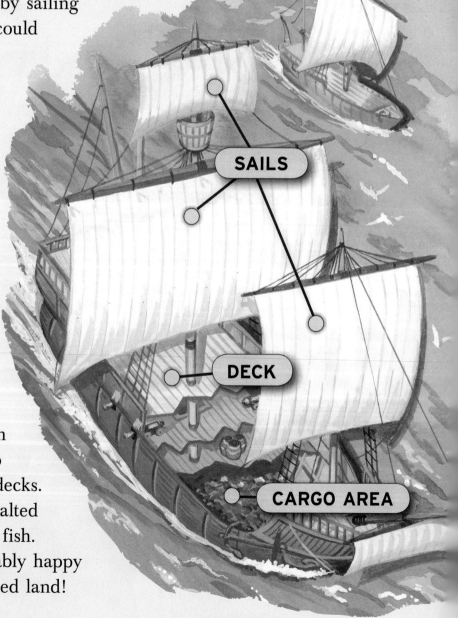

SAILS

DECK

CARGO AREA

Structured Vocabulary Discussion

As your teacher says each vocabulary word, write all the words the vocabulary word makes you think of. When your teacher says "Stop," exchange papers with a partner and explain your words to each other.

Throughout the week, add to your vocabulary journal entries. Record new insights and other words that relate to this week's vocabulary.

Picture It

Copy this chart into your vocabulary journal. Write a definition for **foreign** after the word. Then write words that are and are not examples of **foreign**.

foreign	
Examples	**Non-Examples**
kangaroo	cow

Copy this web into your vocabulary journal. Fill in the circles with reasons why an **explorer** would travel.

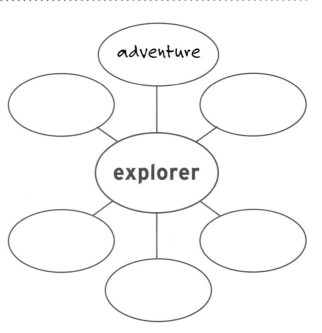

adventure

explorer

Comprehension Strategy

Determine Importance
Purpose for Reading

Your purpose for reading will help you decide what is the important information in a text. Keep your purpose for reading in mind to separate the important information from the unimportant. The importance of information can change according to your purpose for reading.

Information can be **IMPORTANT** or not important based on why you are reading.

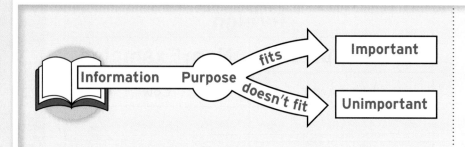

Decide whether information is important or not based on your purpose for reading.

TURN AND TALK Listen to your teacher read the following lines from *Christopher Columbus*. With a partner reread the lines and discuss the following questions.

• What might be a purpose for reading *Christopher Columbus*?

• What information in the passage is most important to that purpose?

Christopher Columbus and most other people during his time knew the earth was round, but they didn't know how big it was. They had always traveled east to get to the Indies. Columbus thought that he could get there more quickly by sailing in the opposite direction.

Christopher asked King John II for three ships to make the voyage. The king refused him.

TAKE IT WITH YOU Next time you read a selection, decide what is the most important information as you read and how it relates to your purpose for reading. Use a chart like the one below to help you.

Purpose for Reading _I want to know how Columbus got to America._

Information That I Noticed	My Purpose for Reading Tells Me It Is...
Christopher was tall and had freckles.	**Important** **Unimportant**
Columbus decided to sail west on the Atlantic Ocean, instead of traveling east over land to the Indies.	**Important** **Unimportant**

The Return of Ponce de León

by Colin Tracy

Characters

Narrator

Juan Ponce de León, *Explorer*

Enrique Ledesma, *ship captain*

Miguel, *a young sailor*

Setting: The characters are standing on the deck of the *San Pedro*, looking out over the Atlantic ocean.

Narrator: In the early 1500s, the explorer Ponce de León sailed to Florida and claimed it for Spain. He now returns to start a new colony there.

Ponce: It won't be long now. Soon we will see the beautiful land of Florida.

Ledesma: Will we go ashore right away?

Ponce: No. We must sail north along the coast to find the perfect place to start our colony.

Miguel: *(to Ponce, shyly)* Sir, do you think we might find the Fountain?

Ledesma: Miguel, you know that's only a story.

Miguel: But sir, don't you believe in the Fountain of Youth?

Ponce: We have orders from the king to make a colony for the glory of Spain. If we find this Fountain along the way, I won't be disappointed.

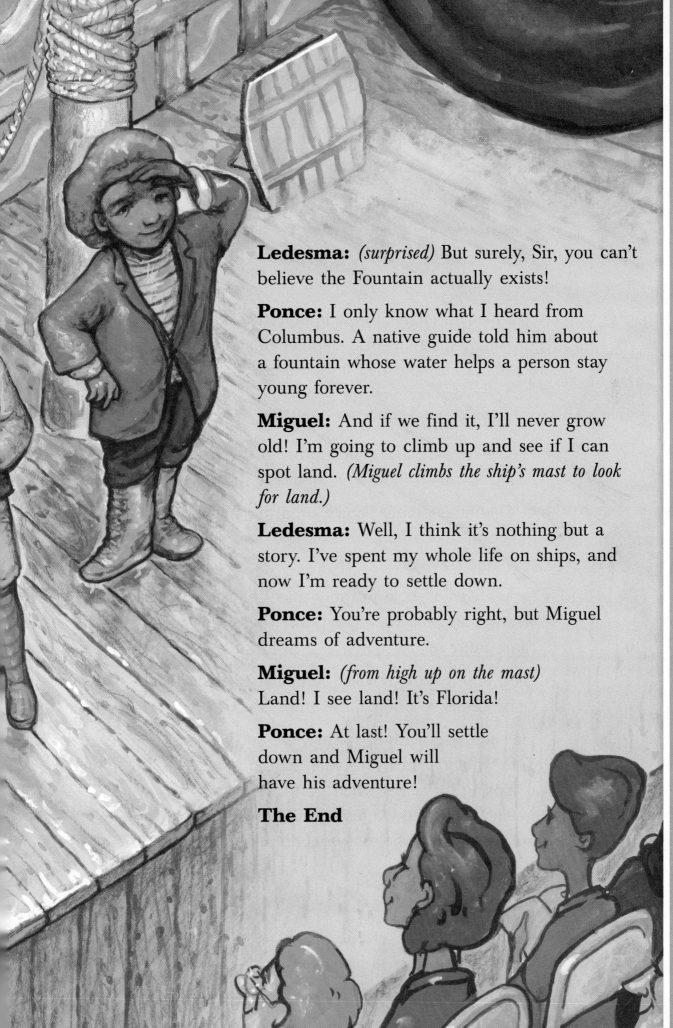

Ledesma: *(surprised)* But surely, Sir, you can't believe the Fountain actually exists!

Ponce: I only know what I heard from Columbus. A native guide told him about a fountain whose water helps a person stay young forever.

Miguel: And if we find it, I'll never grow old! I'm going to climb up and see if I can spot land. *(Miguel climbs the ship's mast to look for land.)*

Ledesma: Well, I think it's nothing but a story. I've spent my whole life on ships, and now I'm ready to settle down.

Ponce: You're probably right, but Miguel dreams of adventure.

Miguel: *(from high up on the mast)* Land! I see land! It's Florida!

Ponce: At last! You'll settle down and Miguel will have his adventure!

The End

Word Study

In Search of SPICE

vanilla beans

It's hard to imagine how important spices were 500 years ago. Today, spices such as pepper, cinnamon, and nutmeg are easy to find and cost little money. But at the time of Columbus's famous voyage, some spices were more valuable than gold. Why?

- People did not have refrigerators 500 years ago. They added spices to food so it wouldn't spoil.

- In Columbus's time, people used many foreign spices as medicine. Cinnamon, for example, was supposed to help heal sore throats!

- People weren't able to grow spices easily in Europe. The weather and soil were not right. That's why most spices came from Asia.

- Long ago, people traveled long distances on sailing ships or by camel to bring spices from Asia.

For all these reasons, spices were very expensive in Europe. People who sold them became rich and powerful. Columbus was looking for spices when he made his famous trip in 1492. He believed he knew a faster route to Asia. What he didn't know was that a whole new world lay in his path.

ginger

cinnamon

cloves

334

Contractions

Activity One

About Contractions

A contraction combines two words to make one word by leaving out one or more letters. An apostrophe in the contraction shows where letters have been left out. For example, *should not* is *shouldn't* and *we are* is *we're*. Listen for contractions as your teacher reads *In Search of Spice*.

Contractions in Context

Read *In Search of Spice* with a partner. Record any contractions you find in the left column of a chart like this one. Then, in the right column of the chart, write the word or words from which each contraction is made.

CONTRACTION	WORDS THAT FORM THE CONTRACTION
it's	it + is

Activity Two

Explore Words Together

Work with a partner to make each word pair on the right into a contraction. List the contractions you made and be ready to share them with the rest of the class.

let us	you are
is not	she is
he will	there is

Activity Three

Explore Words in Writing

Choose three contractions from your list. Write a sentence using each one. Then share your favorite sentence with a partner.

vanilla extract

black pepper

Jessie Oonark: Inuit Artist

by Gail Riley

When you make a piece of art, what inspires you? Do you draw from experiences you have had, places you have been, or people you know? Artist Jessie Oonark got her inspiration from her culture. Jessie was born an Inuit. The Inuit are a civilization who have lived in Canada since before European explorers arrived. Although many influences can be seen in Jessie's work, she's often remembered as an artist who captured the spirit of the Inuit people.

An Old Culture in a New World

The Inuit ancestors of Jessie Oonark grew up in rough, icy land. The area where the Inuit historically have lived is vast. It reaches from Russia, across Alaska and Northern Canada, all the way to Greenland. For many hundreds of years, the Inuit survived as hunters. They moved often in search of food. They often traveled with dog sleds across snow and ice.

What is your purpose for reading this selection?

Explorers from Europe

Starting in the 1500s, European civilization came to the land of the Inuit. Some Europeans were looking for an ocean route to the riches of Asia. The ocean route they hoped for, called the Northwest Passage, did not exist. Many Europeans stayed in northern Canada, where the Inuit lived.

What information is important in this section?

At first, the Europeans and the Inuit did not get along. Over time, the Inuit and the Europeans began to share many parts of their cultures with one another. European explorers and settlers brought cotton thread and wool to the Inuit in the 1800's. They also brought some of their own art. The thread, wool, and art would influence Jessie Oonark's artwork many years later.

Baker Lake, Canada

Read, Cover, Remember, Retell Technique With a partner, take turns reading as much text as you can cover with your hand. Then cover up what you read and retell the information to your partner.

A Challenge for Jessie

Jessie was born around 1906. Her family lived in a community with other Inuit. The freezing temperatures made their lives hard. They fished for food. Whales and caribou—large deer—were important for food, too. These animals also provided materials the Inuit used to make clothing and shelter.

When Jessie was young, she married a man named Quablunnac. Sadly, Quablunnac died in 1953. Without Quablunnac to hunt for the family, they had little to eat. Jessie and her children got help from relatives, but times were hard for everyone. There were not many caribou left to hunt and food was scarce. Jessie needed a way to care for herself and her children.

A Move and a Plan

In 1955, Jessie moved her family to a settlement called Baker Lake. Many other Inuit lived there. She did what she could to earn money. She became a seamstress, making parkas and other clothing to sell at a store in the community.

What information do you learn about Jessie Oonark? Why is that information important?

Getting Started

One day, Jessie went to visit her children's classroom. She watched students as they created drawings. Jessie knew she was skilled and talented with her hands. A new idea was born! She'd start making pictures of her own.

A scientist named Dr. Andrew MacPherson was working near Jessie's home. He found out that she was interested in drawing. Dr. MacPherson made sure that Jessie had paper and pencils for her artwork.

> Why does the author mention Dr. Andrew MacPherson?

A Love for Art

Jessie didn't just experiment with creating art. She blazed forward in her new career. She often created forty or fifty drawings in a single week. Soon she began creating wall hangings and other kinds of art, too. Many of Jessie's works show animals and people.

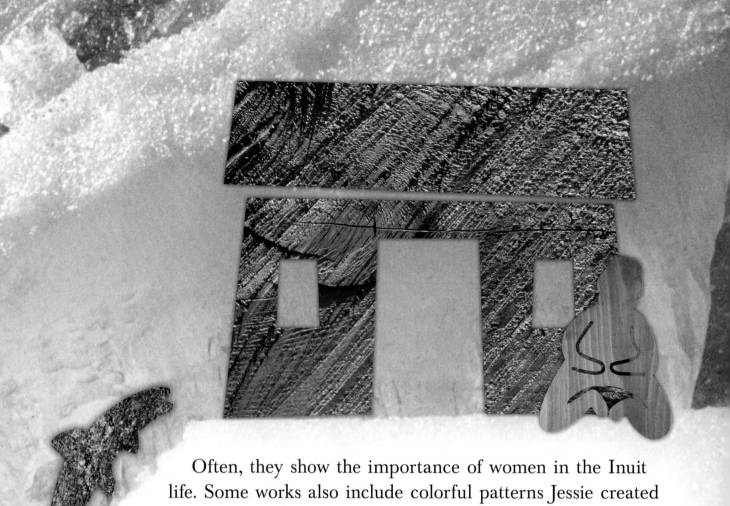

Often, they show the importance of women in the Inuit life. Some works also include colorful patterns Jessie created using traditional Inuit sewing styles. People can look into the life of the Inuit through Jessie Oonark's work.

Jessie quickly became known for her skill and creativity. People began to buy her pieces. Early on, she sold her art through the store in Baker Lake. Before long, however, her art was being seen and sold across the world. It hung in museums. Pictures of her art works were published in books. Jessie won awards.

A Lasting Gift

Jessie Oonark passed away in 1985. Her work is shown and sold at the Jessie Oonark Centre. The Centre is located in Baker Lake and shows Jessie's work. The Centre celebrated its tenth anniversary in 2002. It is also home to a group of Inuit artists who create art in Jessie's style. People around the world can still appreciate and learn about Jessie and the Inuit culture.

What is interesting but unimportant information on this page? Explain.

Think and Respond

Reflect and Write

- You and your partner have read *Jessie Oonark: Inuit Artist* and retold parts of it. Discuss your retellings with your partner. Choose two examples of important information. On one side of an index card, write the important information. On the other side of the index card, write how your purpose for reading helped you decide it was important.

Contractions in Context

Search through *Jessie Oonark* to find contractions. List the contractions. Write the two words each contraction comes from. Then write the letter or letters that were left out of the contraction.

Turn and Talk

DETERMINE IMPORTANCE: PURPOSE FOR READING

Discuss with a partner what you have learned so far about how to read for a purpose.

- How can you determine what is the most important information?
- How does determining the most important information help you to understand text better?

With a partner, reread *Jessie Oonark: Inuit Artist*. Discuss how your purpose for reading helped you decide which information is important information.

Critical Thinking

With a partner discuss how Jessie Oonark's culture is connected to the European explorers. Record your ideas. Look back through the passage to add important ideas from the selection. Then discuss these questions.

- At the time that Jessie Oonark lived, how had the relationship between the Inuit and Europeans changed?
- How was Jessie Oonarks's art a result of Inuit and European culture?

Historian Visits Local School

Cape Cod, MA, November 22 – Tom Hill, a member of the Wampanoag tribe, visited Briggs School last week. He came to the school's celebration of the **anniversary** of the first Thanksgiving.

"I am a member of the Wampanoag, the tribe that greeted the Pilgrims in 1621," Mr. Hill explained. "I have studied the Wampanoag. I am a **historian** for my people."

Mr. Hill explained how the Pilgrims left their **civilization** in Europe for life in the New World. Their **passage** across the sea was long and difficult.

"When the Pilgrims arrived in 1620, it was winter," Hill said. "Many died in the cold, harsh weather. The Wampanoag knew how to keep warm, grow vegetables, catch fish, and hunt animals. The Wampanoag taught the Pilgrims many **valuable** lessons about how to live in this new land. In October 1621, the Pilgrims had a feast and invited the Wampanoag to join them.

One fourth-grade student, Nina, asked Mr. Hill, "What did people eat at the first Thanksgiving?"

"They ate wild turkeys, deer, and rabbit," Mr. Hill explained. "They also ate lobster, clams, and mussels. The meal was a lot different from what you might eat at a Thanksgiving meal today!"

anniversary valuable civilization passage historian

Structured Vocabulary Discussion

With a partner, complete the following questions about your vocabulary words.

- What would be something *valuable* you would take on a long *passage* across the sea?

- What kind of *civilization* might a *historian* write about?

- What is an important *anniversary* of our country?

Throughout the week, add to your vocabulary journal entries. Record new insights and other words that relate to this week's vocabulary.

Picture It

Make a web like this one in your vocabulary journal. Give examples of things you consider **valuable**.

valuable

sports trophy

Create a chart like this one in your vocabulary journal. List activities that a **historian** might do.

historian
read books

343

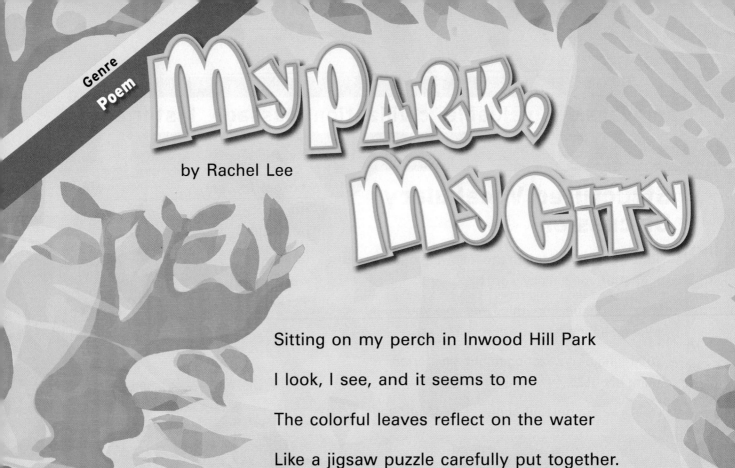

My Park, My City

by Rachel Lee

Sitting on my perch in Inwood Hill Park

I look, I see, and it seems to me

The colorful leaves reflect on the water

Like a jigsaw puzzle carefully put together.

Could these be the trees Henry Hudson saw

As he sailed his ship up New York's shore?

These rocks I rest on with my friends—

Did Hudson also rest from his long passage here?

When Hudson and his men walked ashore

Did the native people stop and stare?

There were no skyscrapers here at the time

Of Hudson's arrival in 1609.

Where wigwams once stood, with bark walls and dirt floors,

Today we build houses, our schools, and huge stores.

Did Hudson use Columbia Rock to guide the way

As a traveler might use our street signs today?

This is my park! This is my city!

It's fun to think of its history—

But now I want to run and play

Free as a bird, and get going with my day.

Ever wonder how early sailors knew where they were going?

Come see our

Mariner's Map Collection

and find out for yourself!

The Mariner's Museum has a huge collection of maps from the Age of Exploration. We have more than 5,000 charts, maps, and pictures to help you understand this important time in history.

Learn about how maps are made and how mapmakers helped Europeans explore the New World. For example, did you know that North and South America are named after Amerigo Vespucci, an Italian mapmaker? He created many maps of the New World and signed his name to each one. After seeing the maps, many people began to call the continents of the New World "America."

The maps at our museum take you on a trip through time. Set sail through 500 years of history. Visit today!

Location:

100 Museum St.

Newport News, VA 23606

Hours:

Mon.–Sat. 10 A.M. to 5 P.M.

Sun. 12 P.M. to 5 P.M.

For more information, contact Mr. Brett Gonzales at 1-555-SEE-MAPS.

Abbreviations

Activity One

About Abbreviations

An abbreviation is a shortened form of a word or phrase. You can use abbreviations for many titles, such as *Mr.* for *Mister*. You may use abbreviations for the names of states in addresses, such as *TX* for *Texas*. Follow along as your teacher reads the flyer aloud and look for abbreviations.

Abbreviations in Context

Read the flyer with a partner. List all the abbreviations you find. Write the abbreviations in the left column of a chart like the one below. Then, in the right column, write what each abbreviation stands for. You may use a dictionary.

ABBREVIATION	WHAT THE ABBREVIATION STANDS FOR
St.	Street

Activity Two

Explore Words Together

April	Avenue
United States	doctor
quart	South Dakota

Work with a partner to change each group of words on the right to an abbreviation. List all your abbreviations. Be ready to share them and their meanings with the rest of the class.

Activity Three

Explore Words in Writing

Write a short letter to a friend or to someone in your family. Use at least three abbreviations in your letter. Then exchange letters with a partner. Read your partner's letter and circle the abbreviations.

EXPLORING THE EXPLORERS

by Joy Nolan

I nearly tripped over a muddy boot just inside the front door. That meant Mom was home from work. "Hi," I called up the stairs. I could hear the fast, quiet clicking of her computer keyboard.

"Hello, Adria," she said. "Come up! It was an exciting day on the ship. Let me tell you about it."

I bounded up, excited to hear her news. My mom is an archeologist. She is working on digging up a ship that sank more than 300 years ago in a bay near our home. The last time Mom said she had good news, I got to go see the ship myself.

Do you know what an *archeologist* does? How could you find out more?

In the 1600s, a Frenchman, Ledoux, arrived in our bay and anchored the ship. He went ashore to build shelter. A bad storm broke out and the ship sank, down through 18 feet of water, deep into the mud. That same kind of gooey, gray mud was on Mom's boots in the hall.

When I walked into my mom's office, she said, "Guess what we might uncover from the ship tomorrow? A *sailor*."

How is the explorer Ledoux like others you have read about?

"You really think there's a skeleton in that old ship?" I asked.

Mom explained that the muck had preserved many valuable things from the ship. "We found a ring and a buckle in the mud. There's a chance we might find bones nearby. Want to come to the dig site? Tomorrow is Saturday."

"*Definitely.*"

Say Something Technique Take turns reading a section of text, covering it up, and then saying something about it to your partner. You may say any thought or idea that the text brings to mind.

I had been to the dig site just once before. It was incredible. The workers had built a ring-shaped dam around the ship. Then they had pumped out the water so the archeologists could work as if they were on dry land. Imagine being aboard a 17th century sunken ship. It was creepy!

On my previous visit, Mom had arranged for me to help other volunteers screening mud. The mud was filled with objects from the ship. We poured water over the mud on the screens and collected what we found. There were coins, glass beads, axe heads, and more—all things the explorers used and traded with the Native Americans that lived in the area.

I was eager to see it all again, maybe even to see a real skeleton!

Describe a place that made you feel excited and nervous. Why did you feel that way?

On Saturday the wind was blowing and it was foggy. By the time we got to the site, the fog had cleared. I could see more of the ship than my last visit. The wood looked old and wet, and it was. Workers kept the wood covered with wet burlap to keep it from drying out and rotting.

Dr. Liu, a historian on the boat, explained that this ship was in the bay only because Ledoux had become lost while looking for the mouth of the Mississippi River.

Mom and I walked over to where a group of scientists were digging slowly. I craned my neck to see. A minute later, a man named Mr. Martin came over and broke the news: there were no bones in that part of the ship. They had been searching for hours and found nothing.

I could tell my mom was disappointed. "That's too bad," she said, looking at me. "It was a long shot anyway. Bones don't last long underwater, even in thick mud like this."

Mom rubbed my head a little. She knew how much I had wanted to see a skeleton.

Does this story of discovery remind you of something else you have seen or heard?

I wanted to go home, but I knew Mom had to work. So I went back to screening mud again. Soon I had found a coin, some pins, and even a knife.

All of a sudden, I heard yelling. "Look what we found," said one of the scientists. He held up a beautiful golden mug. It was engraved "C. Barange."

"Wow, look at that," Mom smiled as she studied the mug. "It's not as exciting as finding a skeleton," she told me, "but it's better in some ways. The mug might have belonged to an important person. With this name, we might find lots more clues about Ledoux and his voyage."

By the time we headed back to town in the evening, I was ready for food, a shower, and some sleep. But even though I was tired, wet, and excited, I wanted to learn more about C. Barange and the real people who had been on the ship. Who were they? What had inspired them to make such a dangerous journey? Now, *that* was something to think about!

What other selections have you read that told about explorers? How is this selection different?

352

Think and Respond

Reflect and Write

- You and your partner have read *Exploring the Explorers* and said something about what you were thinking. Discuss your thoughts with your partner.

- Choose two connections you could make between something you have read, seen, or heard and the story. On one side of an index card, write the connection you made. On the other side, explain the connection.

Abbreviations in Context

Search through *Exploring the Explorers* for abbreviations. List the abbreviations and share them with a partner. Write a paragraph about explorers. Use three or more abbreviations in your paragraph.

Turn and Talk

MAKE CONNECTIONS: TEXT TO TEXT, SELF, AND WORLD

Discuss with a partner what it means to make connections as you are reading.

- How does making connections help you?

Think about the connections you have made in *Exploring the Explorers*. Talk about your connections with a partner. Explain your thinking.

Critical Thinking

In a group, talk about what archaeologists might look for. Create a list of what they might find. Return to *Exploring the Explorers* and check your list against the items found on the sunken ship. Then discuss these questions.

- What does it mean to be a special kind of explorer, such as an archaeologist?

- How do items that scientists find in their digging help them solve puzzles?

- How do you think Adria might find out more about the mug of C. Barange?

In a story, an author writes about made-up, or fictional, characters, settings, and events. In this story, Haru writes about a boy, his uncle, and their amazing discovery.

A Chance Discovery
by Haru Sato

My uncle Pete is an archaeologist. My jaw dropped when he invited me to join him in Mexico and be in his latest article: "Unearthing a Lost Mayan City," by Dr. Pete Solinsky. *Unearthing? Lost cities?* This was perfect for me!

The writer establishes a situation and introduces the characters.

"Do you really think we'll discover ancient ruins?" I asked.

"That's the plan," said Uncle Pete. "However, we're not the only ones looking."

"I'll make a great explorer," I said. "I'm completely fearless! Those other researchers don't stand a chance."

The writer uses dialogue to develop events and characters.

"I know you will, Chris," laughed Uncle Pete.

That was over a week ago. Since then, we've hit some snags. I haven't showered in three days. I found a lizard sleeping on my toothbrush. My palms are sweaty and my skin itches. I've been on the constant lookout for danger and doom. Ah, the life of an explorer!

The writer uses first-person point of view to make the story feel personal.

The jungle is thick and muggy, and Uncle Pete constantly reminds me to watch where I'm going. He reminds me to keep up. He reminds me that a lost city could be buried right under our noses. It all seems pretty hopeless, if you ask me.

Uncle Pete is telling me about ancient Mayan culture, and my mind begins to wander. I imagine air conditioning. I shut my eyes. Then, suddenly, I feel myself falling! I slide downward in the dark and land with a thud.

> The writer uses strong verbs, precise nouns, and descriptive words to describe the action in the story.

"Chris!" yells Uncle Pete.

"I'm OK," I mutter.

"You really are fearless!" he says. "Hang on while I lower a rope."

"Hey, this hole stretches out forever!" I yell.

Uncle Pete grabs his flashlight and shines it down at me. He sees the stone ruins beside me and smiles.

> The writer includes a strong ending for the story—including a solution to the problem.

"Not the most graceful way of doing things," he says. "But I think you've just made an incredible discovery!"

Respond in Writing

Answer these questions about the story you just read.

- What problem does the main character of this story face? How is the problem resolved? Use details from the story to support your answer.

- Does the writer do a good job of describing events and painting a picture for readers? Use words and details from the story to explain why or why not.

Writing: Story

Use the steps of the writing process to create your own story.
The following tips can help make your writing its best.

Prewriting

- Create a list of ideas for your story and choose the one you are most interested in writing about.

- Make notes about the problem you will include in your story.

- Plan how your character will act and change over the course of the story.

- Think about the five senses to list details about your setting.

Drafting

- Begin your story with an interesting event or statement.

- Set the scene by showing instead of telling.

- Consult your prewriting often so that you include details you planned and build tension throughout your story.

- Use dialogue to develop characters and events in your story.

Revising

- Look for places where you can include sensory details to paint a clearer picture for readers.

- Break up any big blocks of "telling" by changing it to dialogue and action.

- Try changing the narrator's point of view to make your story more interesting.

Editing

- Check your story to make sure you've used subject and object pronouns correctly.

- Look for contractions in your work and make sure you have written them correctly.

- Make sure you have used correct formatting and punctuation for any titles you have mentioned.

- Exchange stories with a partner and look for errors in each other's work.

Publishing

- Add a creative title to your writing that will hint at what your story is about.

- Add an illustration to your story and share it with friends and family.

Tiger in a Tropical Storm, 1891

Henri Rousseau (1844–1910)

THEME **11** Life in a Rain Forest

THEME **12** Affecting the Rain Forest

Viewing

The artist who painted this picture never saw a real jungle or a rain forest. He visited gardens and looked in books to create his art.

1. What clues tell you that a storm is happening in the painting?

2. Why do you think the artist used the colors he did here?

3. How do you think the artist would have changed his painting if he could have seen the rain forest?

4. How do you think the artist wants you to feel as you look at this picture?

In This UNIT

In this unit you will read about plants and animals of the rain forest. You will also read about ways people can hurt them or help them.

Contents

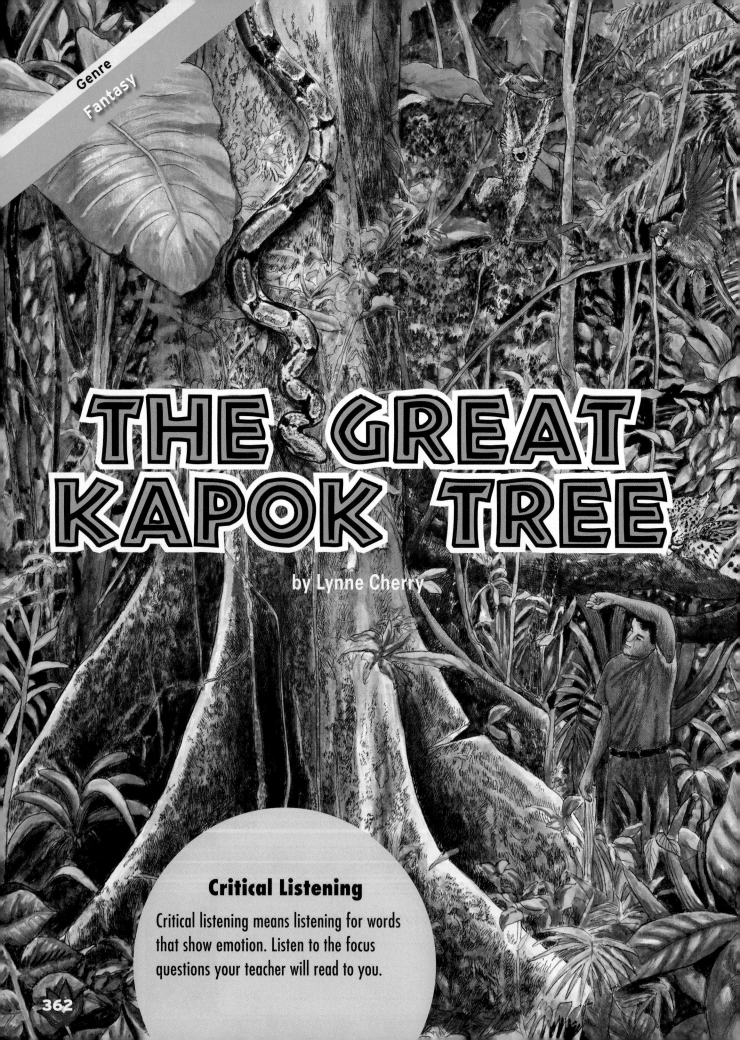

THE GREAT KAPOK TREE

by Lynne Cherry

Critical Listening

Critical listening means listening for words
that show emotion. Listen to the focus
questions your teacher will read to you.

362

Life in Layers

The rain forest is home to half of the world's plants and animals. Each **zone**, or layer, of a rain forest, is different. Different plants and animals live in different zones of the rain forest.

Canopy

The tallest trees form the canopy of a rain forest. The canopy gets the most sunlight, wind, and rain. Toucans and howler monkeys live here. You may see lazy sloths **suspended** from tree limbs. There is so much food in the canopy that some animals, like the sloth, never reach the forest floor.

Understory

The canopy shades the understory. There is little sunlight, so plants do not grow very tall. The air is warm and wet. Snakes and lizards **slither** among the trees. The poison arrow frog lives here, too. It is an unusual **organism**. This frog is tiny, but you can't miss its bright red color with blue spots.

Forest Floor

The forest floor is very dark. Few plants grow here. The floor is covered with leaves, seeds, and twigs that drop from above. Ants, termites, and worms turn these droppings into **nutrients**, or food, for the trees. Large animals such as jaguars, anteaters, and gorillas also live on the floor. People live there, too!

Structured Vocabulary Discussion

Work with a partner or in a small group to fill in the following blanks with a vocabulary word. When you're finished, share your answers with the class. Be sure to explain how the words are connected.

Milk is to *bones* as *nutrients* is to _____.

Sloth is to *suspended* as *snake* is to _____.

> Throughout the week, add to your vocabulary journal entries. Record new insights and other words that relate to this week's vocabulary.

Picture It

Copy this chart into your vocabulary journal. Give examples of a **zone.**

zone
tropics

Copy this word web into your vocabulary journal. In each circle give a different example of an **organism.**

bird — organism

365

Comprehension Strategy !

Infer
Fact/Opinion

A statement of fact can be proven true or false. A statement of opinion is what you believe or feel to be true. Key words and phrases such as *think*, *feel*, *believe*, and *in my opinion* give clues that a statement is an opinion.

A **FACT** is a true statement that can be proved.

An **OPINION** is an idea someone believes about something.

Can it be proved?

To figure out the difference between a fact and an opinion, decide if the statement can be proved true.

TURN AND TALK Listen as your teacher reads these sentences from *The Great Kapok Tree*. Then with a partner, discuss each statement below and decide whether it is a fact or an opinion. Use these questions to help you.

• Can you do research to figure out if the statement is true or false?

• Do you see key opinion words, such as *think*, *feel*, or *believe*?

• Many people settle on the land. They set fires to clear the underbrush, and soon the forest disappears.

• Senhor, this tree is a tree of miracles.

• Senhor, my hive is in this Kapok tree, and I fly from tree to tree and flower to flower collecting pollen.

• He does not think of his own children, who tomorrow must live in a world without trees.

366

TAKE IT WITH YOU As you read other selections, ask yourself whether you could prove each statement true or false. Use a chart like the one below to help you.

In the Text	Can You Prove It? How?	Fact or Opinion?
"Senhor, this tree is a tree of miracles."	No, you can not prove this is a tree of miracles.	☑ Fact ✔ **Opinion**
"Many people settle on the land."	Yes, this could be proved by doing research.	✔ **Fact** ☑ Opinion

TIGER TALK
What Do You Think?

Many rain forest animals are endangered. However, people have different ideas about how we can help. What do you think? Below are two arguments about how to protect rain forest tigers. Read each one and decide for yourself!

Keep Tigers Safe

by Colin Tracy

The tiger is one of the most beautiful animals in the world. Its orange coat with black stripes makes it one of the most unusual animals of the rain forest. The tiger is the largest predator of the cat family. The Siberian tiger can weigh up to 700 pounds! Tigers live in Asia. They hunt deer and wild pigs.

Sadly, the tiger is one organism in the rain forest that is in danger of disappearing. People cut down the rain forest to build homes and farms. That leaves less room for tigers. People illegally hunt tigers for their fur.

Many organizations have started programs to help save the tiger. Many tigers have found new homes in zoos and preserves.

Zoos provide us with many tools to learn about wildlife. Every time we go to the zoo, we learn more about the tiger. This knowledge is very important if we want to protect tigers for the future.

Tigers Should Live in the Wild

by Theodore Greenberg

There's only one way to help tigers. We must save the land where they live. Large wildlife preserves offer safety for the animals. In a wildlife preserve, animals roam in their natural habitat. They hunt and raise their young on their own.

World Tiger Population

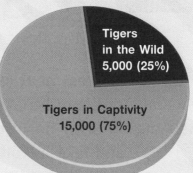

Tigers in the Wild 5,000 (25%)

Tigers in Captivity 15,000 (75%)

Can zoos give tigers what a preserve can give them? Tigers need large areas of land to find food. Zoos do not give tigers large spaces to move around. In fact, you often see tigers in zoos pace around in circles.

Many people love to watch tigers and their cubs at the zoo. But what happens when the cubs get older? Some zoos sell tigers to private owners. The new owners keep the tigers as pets or for wild animal shows. These tigers sometimes live in unhealthy conditions. If their new homes are in a climate zone that is too hot and dry, the tigers might become sick. Often, it is also hard for owners to provide the nutrients tigers need to stay healthy.

Where is the best place for tigers to live? My answer is the best place for tigers is in the wild or in wildlife preserves.

DISCOVERY IN THE AMAZON

by Dr. Mark Ross, Scientist

Madeira River

Brazilian Amazon Basin

May 15 Rain forest near Madeira River, Brazil

My son, Tom, and I took a boat ride on the Madeira River in the Amazon River Basin today. We decided to dock the boat and take a walk into the rain forest. Suddenly, leaves started to drift down from a tree high in the canopy above us. I looked up through my binoculars and saw something I had never seen before. It was a cat-sized monkey with brown fur and a dark orange beard. It had a long black tail with a white tip. We decided to make our camp there that night. "Maybe we'll see more monkeys like these tomorrow!" Tom said excitedly.

May 18 Rain forest near Madeira River, Brazil

Tom's wish came true. We began observing two families of monkeys. Their loud screaming awakened us early each morning. They ate fruit, leaves, and insects. They walked on all four feet in the trees, but sometimes we would see them leap from branch to branch. They never went down to the forest floor. In the middle of the day, the monkeys took a nap in pairs and wrapped their long tails together. Tom took lots of photos. We will use them as proof to show we have found a new type of monkey.

Pronouns

Activity One

About Pronouns

A noun is a word that names a person, place, or thing. A **pronoun** takes the place of a noun. The pronoun *he* can take the place of the noun *Tom*. For example, *Tom* hit the ball. *He* ran to first base. The noun *Tom* is the antecedent for *He*. As your teacher reads *Discovery in the Amazon*, listen for pronouns.

Pronouns in Context

Read *Discovery in the Amazon* with a partner. Record any pronouns you find in the left column of a chart like this one. Then, in the right column of the chart, write the noun that the pronoun replaces.

PRONOUN	ANTECEDENT NOUN
I	Dr. Ross

Activity Two

Explore Words Together

Work with a partner to think of nouns that could replace the pronouns shown on the right. List your nouns and be ready to share them with the class.

I	we
she	they
he	it

Activity Three

Explore Words in Writing

Write a journal entry telling what you learned about the rain forest today. Include at least two pronouns. Share your journal entry with a partner.

Walking on the Treetops

by Julia LoFaso

"Felicia," Dad squeezes my shoulder, "this is going to be your best winter break ever."

I think he might be right! Today is our first day in the country of Peru, and soon we'll be in Iquitos (E-key-tos), a small city in the heart of the Amazon rain forest. Dad lives here for three months of the year. He is a biologist, a kind of scientist that studies plants and animals. I'll only be here for a week, but he has many activities planned.

Dad and I stand near a dock with our group, waiting for a boat to take us down the Amazon River. The river, Dad explains, is two miles wide in some places.

"Our first stop is the rain forest floor," he tells me, "where we'll be surrounded by lush, green plants."

"Dad," I giggle, "you sound like the tour book I read on the plane." He smiles.

"What else will we do?" I ask. "Everything sounds incredible."

"We will see rare, gorgeous birds like the red cotinga. We may visit a Yanomami village. But the most unforgettable thing," Dad tells me, "will be a walk on the treetops!"

> What kinds of things does Felicia learn from her father as they wait for the boat?

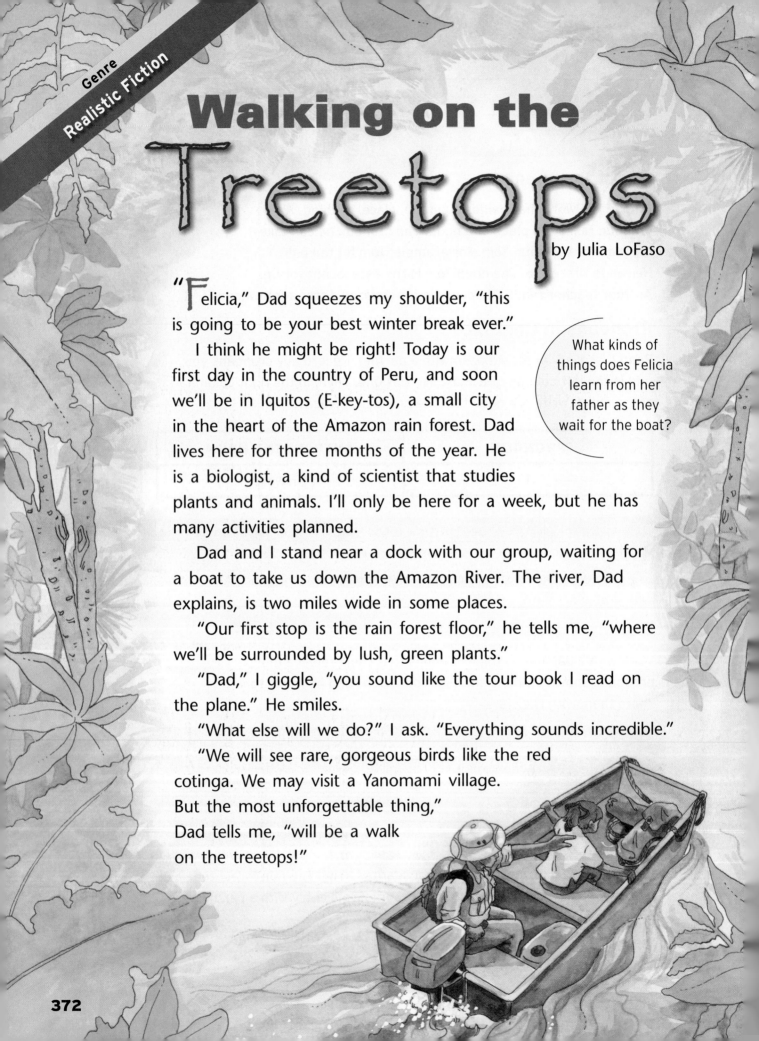

"What's that?" I ask nervously.

Dad explains that above the trees in the rain forest's canopy, a complex system of bridges was built so people can look down on the rain forest.

"And how high is this walkway?" I ask.

"At least ten stories!" Dad answers. "The view is amazing." I try to look excited, but I'm terrified.

"Look, Felicia," Dad points off into the distance.

I follow his finger and notice dolphins jumping from the water in perfect semi-circles. "They're really cool!" I shout.

"One is a gray river dolphin and one is a pink river dolphin," he tells me. "They live in the river."

"I love how the water sparkles," I say. "It's beautiful."

"It looks even more impressive from way up in the canopy." He winks at me.

I give him a shaky smile and try not to think about being up that high.

Find one fact about the dolphins on this page. Then find one opinion.

Read, Cover, Remember, Retell Technique
With a partner, take turns reading as much text as you can cover with your hand. Then cover up what you read and retell the information to your partner.

We arrive in the rain forest by afternoon. The ground is moist. High above us, dark green leaves block out the sun, moss clings to tree trunks, and vines tangle around everything.

I wake up at dawn the next morning. Rain forest animals squawk and jabber around us as we eat breakfast. Suddenly, I hear a loud croak.

"Is that a frog?" I ask Dad.

Dad listens. "Nope, it's a toucan. Their call is similar to a frog's, but toucans are birds. Sometimes toucans eat small frogs though."

"Do they hunt any other prey?" I ask.

Dad nods. "They also capture and eat insects."

"Do you think we'll see one?" I ask.

"We might," he answers, "they live in the canopy."

Dad explains that the rain forest is a complex environment. Since there isn't much light near the forest floor, only certain plants and animals survive. But up in the canopy, where we're going, there are lots of birds and monkeys that feed on nuts and fruit.

Name three facts you learned about the rain forest on this page.

With our group, Dad and I hike toward the canopy walkway. When we arrive at the entrance to the walkway, I look up. It's a towering wooden staircase and I want to turn around. It has to be higher than three ferris wheels and it looks like there are about fifteen million steps to the top!

Dad pats me on the back. "Keep your eyes on the steps. I promise I'll be right behind you the entire time."

On the damp rain forest floor, I take a deep breath to relax. Then I follow Dad.

As we climb, I keep my eyes on the walkway. Dad calls out, "Hey Felicia! How much soup does a toucan eat for lunch?"

"I don't know, Dad. How much?"

"Two cans!" Dad laughs hysterically.

"Dad!" I groan, "First, you already explained what toucans eat. Second, that's a ridiculous joke!" I chuckle, and then I realize that I'm not terrified anymore. I also notice that we've almost reached the top of the staircase.

> What is Felicia's opinion about her dad's joke? How do you know it is an opinion?

"OK," Dad says, "We've made it to the canopy walkway! Now we'll be walking on a series of flat platforms, grasping the ropes on either side. Are you ready to see something amazing?"

I gulp. "I guess so," I say.

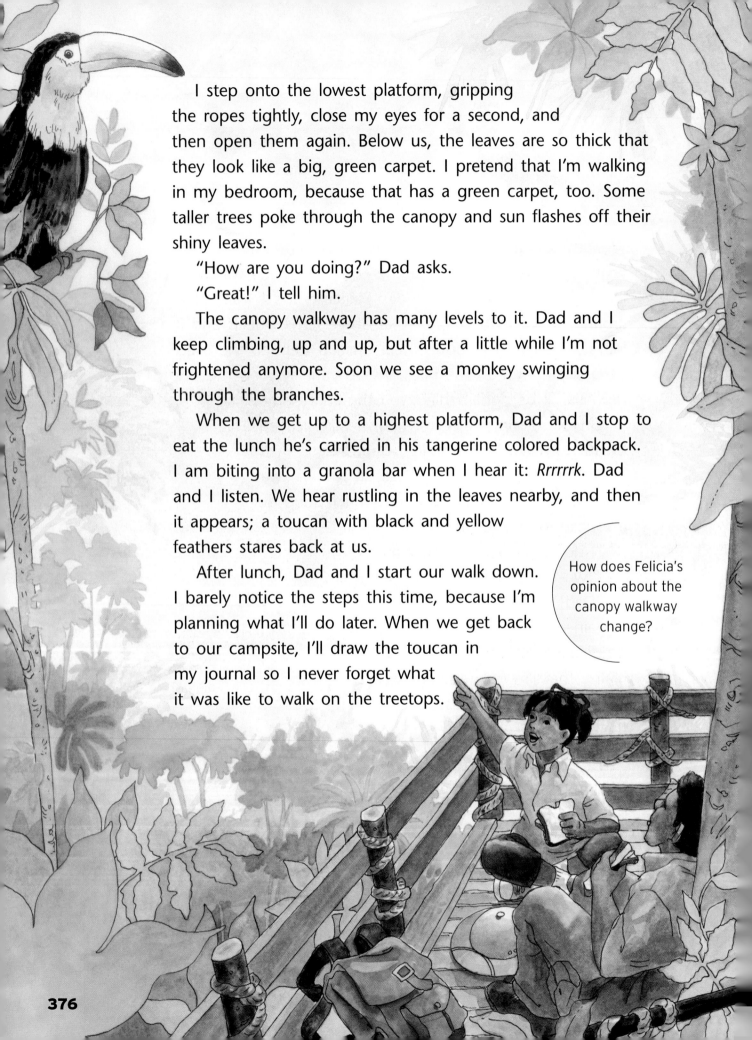

I step onto the lowest platform, gripping the ropes tightly, close my eyes for a second, and then open them again. Below us, the leaves are so thick that they look like a big, green carpet. I pretend that I'm walking in my bedroom, because that has a green carpet, too. Some taller trees poke through the canopy and sun flashes off their shiny leaves.

"How are you doing?" Dad asks.

"Great!" I tell him.

The canopy walkway has many levels to it. Dad and I keep climbing, up and up, but after a little while I'm not frightened anymore. Soon we see a monkey swinging through the branches.

When we get up to a highest platform, Dad and I stop to eat the lunch he's carried in his tangerine colored backpack. I am biting into a granola bar when I hear it: *Rrrrrrk*. Dad and I listen. We hear rustling in the leaves nearby, and then it appears; a toucan with black and yellow feathers stares back at us.

After lunch, Dad and I start our walk down. I barely notice the steps this time, because I'm planning what I'll do later. When we get back to our campsite, I'll draw the toucan in my journal so I never forget what it was like to walk on the treetops.

How does Felicia's opinion about the canopy walkway change?

Think and Respond

Reflect and Write

- You and your partner have read *Walking on the Treetops*. Discuss what you retold to each other.

- Write three facts from the story on one side of an index card. On the other side write three opinions. Exchange your cards with your partner. Did you write the same facts and opinions? Discuss your choices.

Pronouns in Context

Search through *Walking on the Treetops* to find as many pronouns as you can. Write down the pronouns and the nouns they stand for.

Turn and Talk

INFER: FACT/OPINION

Discuss with a partner what you have learned so far about facts and opinions.

- Why is it important to know the difference between a fact and an opinion?

Think about the story events and the characters. With a partner, discuss the facts and opinions you found. Explain your thinking.

Critical Thinking

In a small group, discuss what Felicia sees and learns on her visit to the Amazon. Write Felicia's opinions at the beginning of the story. Then discuss these questions.

- Did Felicia's opinions change during her visit with her father? Did some of her opinions stay the same?

- How can facts help us with our opinions?

WHAT'S FOR DINNER?

All the plants and animals in a rain forest make up a **complex** ecosystem. They depend upon each other to live and **thrive**. The relationships in this ecosystem can be drawn as a food web.

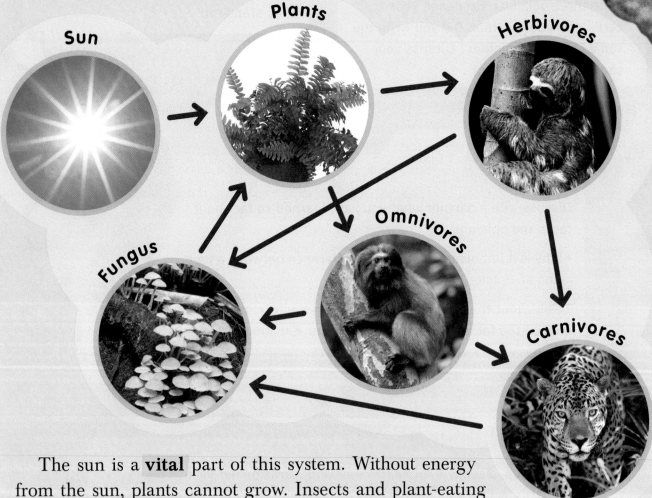

The sun is a **vital** part of this system. Without energy from the sun, plants cannot grow. Insects and plant-eating animals (herbivores) eat the plants. Animals become **prey** for **predators**, animals that hunt other animals. Meat-eating animals are called carnivores. Some animals, called omnivores, eat both plants and animals.

When plants and animals die, they are still part of the food web. Insects, worms, and fungus eat and break down the dead plants and animals. What is left becomes food for plants.

Arrows show how energy moves through the food web.

complex   vital   predator   thrive   prey

Structured Vocabulary Discussion

Work with a partner to complete these sentences about your vocabulary words.

Nutrients are _____ for a person to *thrive*.

Prey and *predator* are related because . . .

Things that are *complex* are . . .

Throughout the week, add to your vocabulary journal entries. Record new insights and other words that relate to this week's vocabulary.

Picture It

Copy this chart into your vocabulary journal. Write down any animal in the rain forest that is a **predator**.

predator
bird

Copy this word web into your vocabulary journal. In the spaces, write any animal in the rain forest that is **prey** for other animals.

insects

prey

Sounds of the Rain Forest

sung to the tune of
"My Bonnie Lies Over the Ocean"
by Becky Manfredini

The animals here are quite busy

As rain falls continuously,

As the lemur glides among the branches,

The monkeys start swinging from tree to tree.

Splish, splash, splish, splash, rat-a-tat-tat,
plip, plop, splash, plip, plop!
Splish, splash, splish, splash, rat-a-tat-tat,
plip, plop, splash!

The hummingbird sips on nectar,

the toucan eats fruit from a tree,

a predator looks for its next meal,

I'm wondering where it might be!

Splish, splash, splish, splash, rat-a-tat-tat,
plip, plop, splash, plip, plop!
Splish, splash, splish, splash, rat-a-tat-tat,
plip, plop, splash!

The rain plops on flowers and branches,

Some animals hide in a tree,

Many will get wet and have fun,

While others will sleep peacefully!

Splish, splash, splish, splash, rat-a-tat-tat,
plip, plop, splash, plip, plop!
Splish, splash, splish, splash, rat-a-tat-tat,
plip, plop, splash!

Letters from the Forest

Dear Lopaka,

Hi, I'm your new pen pal! I live in Portland, Oregon. Most people do not know that Portland is in a rain forest. It's not as hot as other rain forests, but it does rain cats and dogs. We have beautiful trees here, like the Big-leaf Maple and the Sitka Spruce.

Have to get busy with homework now, or I'll have to wing it tomorrow in math. I'm sending pictures of Oregon.

Sincerely,
Robert

Oregon

Dear Robert,

Did you know that your name is "Lopaka" in Hawaiian? We have the same name!
I live on the Hawaiian island of Kauai. We get our share of rain, but we have dry times, too. We have two wet seasons and two dry seasons. But it stays warm all year long.
Have you seen pictures of the tropical rain forest? That's how Hawaii looks, and we have plenty of birds and bugs. Now you've got the news straight from the horse's mouth. Of course, we have modern cities, too.
Guess I'd better sign off. I'm in the same boat you are. I'm up to my ears in math homework!
Anyway, I'm sending you pictures, too.
Your friend,
Lopaka

Hawaii

Idioms

Activity One

About Idioms

An idiom is a phrase that means more than just the words in the idiom. It cannot be understood by simply putting together the meanings of the individual words. Use nearby words and phrases to figure out an idiom's meaning. As your teacher reads *Letters From the Forest*, listen for idioms.

Kauai, Hawaii

Idioms in Context

With a partner, read the pen pals' letters. Make a chart like the one below to show the idioms you find and the meaning of each.

IDIOM	MEANING
rain cats and dogs	rains very hard

Activity Two

Explore Words Together

Work with a partner. Draw a picture to show what the idiom means. Discuss its meaning with classmates. Then, write what the idiom means when people use it.

in a pickle
out on a limb
under the weather
sleep like a log
spill the beans
bells and whistles

Activity Three

Explore Words in Writing

Choose three of the idioms from Activities 1 and 2. Include them in a letter to a friend. Use complete sentences and be sure that your sentences show what each idiom means.

Portland, Oregon

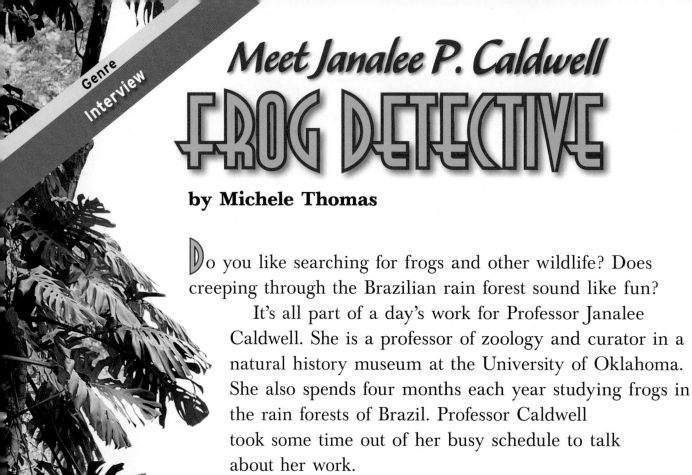

Meet Janalee P. Caldwell
FROG DETECTIVE

by Michele Thomas

Do you like searching for frogs and other wildlife? Does creeping through the Brazilian rain forest sound like fun?

It's all part of a day's work for Professor Janalee Caldwell. She is a professor of zoology and curator in a natural history museum at the University of Oklahoma. She also spends four months each year studying frogs in the rain forests of Brazil. Professor Caldwell took some time out of her busy schedule to talk about her work.

What do you do in the rain forest? How do you do your research?

We have a research team of about 6 people. I don't go it alone. We go to remote areas in the Amazon rain forest and set up a camp.

Every day we go into the forest to find amphibians. We study where they live and what they eat. Most frogs are active at night. So at night we go into the forest. We wear headlights and wade into ponds and swamps where we hear many frogs calling.

What would be your purpose for reading this interview?

Have you ever found a new species of frog?

Scientists are continually finding "new" species of frogs. Of course, the frogs have been there all along. But scientists only find them when they visit areas far away from cities. Every time I go to the rain forest, I find at least 5 to 10 new species. However, I know I have barely scratched the surface.

What are some other things you've discovered?

Recently I made a discovery about one species of poison-dart frogs. I found that the same male and female remain together for a long time. They work together to feed their tadpoles and help them thrive.

The male carries the tadpole on his back after it hatches from an egg. He brings it to a small, water-filled hole in a tree or vine. Then he stays nearby and calls. Every few days, the female answers his calls. The male leads her to the tree hole where the tadpole lives. The female enters the tree hole and lays two eggs. The eggs are vital for the tadpole to survive. The male and female feed their tadpole for about two months until it turns into a frog.

> How does your purpose for reading help you determine the important information on this page?

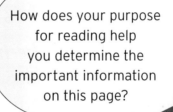

FUN FACTS ABOUT FROGS

- **There are about 3,800 different kinds of frogs.** Many of these are found in rain forests. Many frogs have thin skin that they "breathe" through. They easily lose water through their skin. If they lose too much water, they might die.

- **Frogs typically live in warm, wet places.** In rain forests, many frogs are found on land because of the high humidity and frequent rains.

- **Frogs eat insects.** Tree frogs eat large insects, such as grasshoppers. Some poison-dart frogs eat mostly ants. They may eat up to 400 or so at one time. Other frogs eat termites.

- **Listen for frog calls at night.** Every frog species has a different call. Scientists often use the calls to tell similar species apart.

Reverse Think-Aloud Technique Listen as your partner reads part of the text aloud. Choose a point in the text to stop your partner and ask what he or she is thinking about the text at that moment. Then switch roles with your partner.

What are you working on now?

I have been working on frog calls. I take a digital recorder into the field and record calls. Then I transfer the calls from the recorder to the computer. I have a computer program that makes a diagram of the frog call. Using these diagrams, I compare the calls of different species. I also study how frogs change their calls when another frog is nearby.

What is it like in the rain forest? How do you live there?

We often go to remote areas. We do not have electricity, so we take enough batteries to use flashlights or headlights at night. We take lots of rice, beans, and dried cereal. We construct an open-air camp from small trees and use palm thatch for a roof. We hang hammocks to sleep in.

The best thing is hearing all the frogs, insects, monkeys, and other animal noises at night. The large tarantulas and centipedes that move into the camp with us can sometimes be a little scary.

Why are the fun facts set off from the interview? How do the facts help you understand Prof. Caldwell's work?

What time is best to work in the rain forest?

It is best for me to work in the rainy season. That is when most frogs are active and easily found.

I get used to being wet in the rain. I once wanted to know what some poison-dart frogs did during the rain. I watched one frog for three hours while it rained nearly five inches. I was swamped!

Rainy nights are the most exciting to me because many frogs come out all at once. The ponds are filled with frogs. Their calls are so loud you cannot hear the person next to you.

What it is like to live in the rain forest?

Professor Caldwell sets up a table at her camp to use as a laboratory.

How did you feel about frogs when you were in fourth grade?

Even before the fourth grade, I loved being outside and watching animals. I saw my first snake at age 6. I was very excited and not afraid at all.

I was fascinated with frogs and tadpoles even when I was a little girl. My father brought me a newt (a type of salamander that lives in water). For hours I used to watch it swim in its aquarium and eat tadpoles.

Is the information on this page important? Explain how your purpose for reading helps you decide.

When I was in the fourth grade, I did not know you could become a scientist and study frogs in their habitat. I thought I might become a veterinarian. Luckily, I discovered later that I could study biology!

Professor Caldwell at work in the rain forest.

Think and Respond

Reflect and Write

• You and your partner have read *Janalee P. Caldwell, Frog Detective* and have taken turns expressing your thoughts. Discuss the thoughts you had while you were reading.

• On one side of an index card, write an example of important information from the interview. On the other side, explain how your purpose for reading helped you decide what information was important.

Idioms in Context

Look back through *Meet Janalee P. Caldwell, Frog Detective* for idioms. Discuss with a partner what each idiom means. Then make a list of these and other idioms you know. Write a one-paragraph story about a student who takes a trip to a rain forest. Include as many idioms as you can.

Turn and Talk

DETERMINE IMPORTANCE: PURPOSE FOR READING

Discuss with a partner what you have learned about setting a purpose for reading.

• How does knowing your purpose for reading help you determine the important information in what you read?

Discuss with your partner how your purpose for reading helped you recognize the difference between important and interesting information in *Janalee P. Caldwell, Frog Detective*.

Critical Thinking

With a partner, discuss the challenges for scientists conducting research in the rain forest. Write a list of some of the challenges for Professor Caldwell as she researches frogs in the Brazilian rain forest. Then discuss these questions.

• Why do scientists face challenges to study animals in the rain forest?

• How do you think you might meet the challenges of studying in the rain forest?

In a persuasive essay, an author states an opinion about a topic and urges readers to take action. In this persuasive essay, Marcelina writes about threats to the Amazon rain forest and explains how people can help by reducing, reusing, and recycling.

Do Your Part to Save the Amazon
by Marcelina Olivares

The Amazon rain forest is full of plants and animals found nowhere else on Earth. It is an important source of food and fresh water for animals and people. This amazing South American forest supplies 20 percent of Earth's oxygen. Unfortunately, the rain forest is rapidly shrinking. Many trees have been cut down to be turned into paper and other products. Logging and other human activities are the greatest threats to the rain forest.

The writer clearly introduces the topic for the persuasive essay.

We must do everything we can to stop the destruction of the rain forest. Choices we make every day can help to preserve the rain forest. Each time we choose to reduce, reuse, and recycle, we make a difference. One of the most important things we can do is to reduce the amount of paper we use. For example, use a cloth towel instead of paper towels. Reduce the amount of junk mail your family receives. With a parent's permission, write or email companies to ask them not to send junk mail.

The writer states an opinion and urges readers to take action.

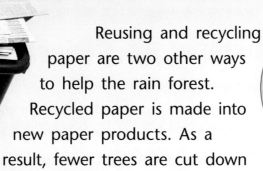

Reusing and recycling paper are two other ways to help the rain forest. Recycled paper is made into new paper products. As a result, fewer trees are cut down to make new products. When you shop, look for packages made from recycled paper. In order to help, we need to think about how each purchase we make impacts the rain forests.

> The writer provides reasons that are supported by facts and details.

Up to 60 percent of the Amazon rain forest may be destroyed in the next 20 years. Ask yourself what steps you can take to protect the rain forest. Everyone will need to go the extra mile. Reducing, reusing, and recycling are a few important things we can do to help. Our actions will mean a brighter future for the rain forests.

> The writer provides a conclusion that summarizes the main idea and convinces readers to act.

Respond in Writing

Answer these questions about the persuasive essay you just read.

- What is the writer's opinion in this persuasive essay? What reasons does the writer include to support her opinion?

- What connecting words or phrases does the writer use to link sentences and ideas in her essay?

Writing: Persuasive Essay

Use the steps of the writing process to create a persuasive essay.
The following tips can help you make your writing its best.

Prewriting

- Think about topics that are important to you and that you have a strong opinion about.

- Write an opinion statement using the word *should*. Make sure your statement clearly tells your audience what you want them to do.

- Write a list of reasons and examples that support your opinion.

Drafting

- Refer to your prewriting as you draft your persuasive essay.

- Begin your essay by getting the reader's attention with a creative opening sentence.

- State your opinion clearly and include strong supporting details.

- Include a call to action, something your readers can do to help solve the problem.

- Think about your audience and purpose as you write. When you ask your audience to take action, make sure it is something that they can do.

Revising

- Check your beginning and ending to make sure your opinion and your call to action work as a team.

- Check that your ideas are grouped together and well organized. Make sure your call to action offers a solution to the problem you've introduced.

- Look for and eliminate exaggerations. Stretching the truth will weaken your argument.

- Remember to use a variety of sentence types to make your writing more interesting.

Editing

- Look for articles in your essay, such as *a*, *an*, and *the*. Make sure you've chosen the correct articles in each sentence.

- Check that you're using the correct form of comparative or superlative adjectives.

- Find places where you used two or more adjectives together. Make sure your adjectives are in the correct order.

- Check for misspelled words. Consult reference materials as needed.

Publishing

- Create a clean copy of your essay.

- Submit your essay to your school paper or to a local newspaper to encourage your community to take action.

Affecting the Rain Forest

Contents

Rickie and Henri

by Jane Goodall

Illustrated by Alan Marks

Appreciative Listening

Appreciative listening means listening for parts of the story you find funny or sad. Listen to the focus questions your teacher will read to you.

Jane Goodall
Friend to Chimpanzees and Forests

Jane Goodall wrote *Rickie and Henri.* She is a scientist who has spent many years studying chimpanzees. Jane's work with chimps began almost fifty years ago in Africa.

At first, Jane would watch the chimps from a distance with binoculars. But gradually the chimps allowed her to come closer. One day to her **bewilderment**, she saw chimps making tools to catch food. This was a big surprise. Before Jane's discovery, scientists believed that only people made tools. **Eventually** Jane made many other discoveries about chimps. For example, she learned that chimps eat meat. She also argued that each chimp has its own personality.

Another important thing Jane learned was that chimps are in danger. People hunt chimps. They also destroy their habitat. She created a protected place called Tchimpounga Sanctuary. Inside the sanctuary, the animals and their habitats are safe from hunters and loggers.

Jane also continues to teach others about chimps and the environment. She gives speeches all around the world. Her work is **beneficial** to the many animals that need protection. Her many efforts **convince** people to protect the chimps and preserve their habitat. Even a small **sacrifice** of time or money can be a big help to chimpanzees in danger.

Structured Vocabulary Discussion

Work in a small group. First, your teacher will say a vocabulary word. Then take turns saying the first word that comes to mind. The last student in your group will say a word that finishes the round. Finally, explain why your word is related to the vocabulary word.

Throughout the week, add to your vocabulary journal entries. Record new insights and other words that relate to this week's vocabulary.

Picture It

Copy this web into your vocabulary journal. Fill in the circles with things that are **beneficial** to animals for their survival.

safe homes

beneficial

Copy this chart into your vocabulary journal. List ways you might **convince** someone to help the chimpanzees.

convince
write a letter

Comprehension Strategy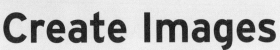

Create Images
Enhance Understanding

As you read, use what you already know and the words you are reading to create images, or pictures in your mind, about the characters and events in a story. This can help you improve your understanding of what the author shows, but does not tell you directly.

Use MENTAL IMAGES to help you understand what you read.

Use your senses and feelings to create mental images that help you understand your reading.

TURN AND TALK Listen to your teacher read the following lines from *Rickie & Henri*. Then, with your partner, discuss the images of Rickie that come to your mind. Answer these questions.

• Which words help you create pictures in your mind?

• What mental images do you have as you read the words?

The hunter seized Rickie and pushed her into a tiny basket, while the infant chimpanzee, who didn't understand, went on screaming and screaming for her mother.

The long journey through the forest, cramped in a little basket, must have been a nightmare for Rickie. She was hungry, but there was no warm, comforting milk. She was frightened. And she was hurting because shotgun pellets were lodged in her little body. But however much she cried, there was no one to help.

TAKE IT WITH YOU Creating mental images helps you understand what you read. It also makes reading more fun! As you read other selections, try to create as many pictures in your mind as you can. Use a graphic organizer like the one below to record words and phrases that help you create pictures in your mind as you read.

In the Text

The hunter grabs Rickie and pushes her into a tiny basket. Rickie is hurt and frightened.

Image in My Mind

 See

darkness

 Hear

screaming
crying

 Taste

thirsty

Touch

cramped tiny basket, shotgun pellets in her body

Smell

her mother's smell

Feel

frightened, hungry, alone

A Letter to Treetop Products, Inc.

3457 Appleton Way
Forestville, Texas 78732

May 7, 2011

Mr. Tom Royal, CEO
Treetop Products, Inc.
P.O. Box 5555
Seattle, WA 98063

Dear Mr. Royal:

I am writing to ask you for information about your company. I am researching companies that make products from trees. I am interested in the effect that their businesses have on the environment. I would like to make my report on your company.

I have learned that Treetops Products is a logging company. I have read that you sell wood and paper products from rain forests all around the world. Does your company do anything to help the trees grow back? Do you know how many trees are cut down each year? Are you doing anything to make sure you are not chopping down too many trees?

Tropical rain forests are very important. If we chop down too many trees, then the rain forests will quickly disappear. We have been studying rain forests in class, and I have learned that the trees in the rain forests absorb carbon dioxide. This helps slow global warming. Twenty percent of the oxygen for the whole world comes from the Amazon rain forest. The rain forests are like the lungs of our planet. Without them, we couldn't breathe!

The rain forest is also filled with plants that are beneficial to humans. Cures and treatments for many illnesses have been discovered in rain forests. Did you know that twenty-five percent of Western medicines come from plants? The rain forests are like giant pharmacies!

There are other uses for rain forest plants as well. Tropical oils, gums, and tree sap are in many products we use. They are used to make pest spray, rubber, fuel, and paint. Oils from tropical trees and plants are used in many beauty products. Do you cut down trees to make any products like these?

My class has learned that each day, hundreds of species of rare plants, animals, and insects are hurt by logging in the rain forest. Do you think that you sacrifice our future with your activities? I hope that your answer is, "No!"

Does your company believe in maintaining one of our most important natural resources? If so, please send me information on how your company preserves the rain forest.

Sincerely yours,

Letitia Alison Whitlow

Mr. Tom Royal, CEO
Treetop Products, Inc.
P.O Box 5555
Seattle, WA 98063

Grammar

BRING THEM BACK!

Jaguar

- Jaguars are the largest cats in the Americas. When hunting, a jaguar quietly stalks, pounces, and swiftly takes down its prey.

- Today, jaguars are rare in this country. They have vanished from 50 percent of the areas in which they once roamed.

- To help save the jaguar, countries such as Brazil and Mexico are creating preserves.

Komodo dragon

- The Komodo dragon is the world's largest living lizard. It can grow up to 12 feet long and weigh 300 pounds! Though large, these dragons can run 20 miles per hour!

- Long ago, Komodo dragons roamed freely on the islands of Indonesia. Today they are endangered.

- Currently, the Indonesian government protects these giant lizards in Komodo National Park.

Drill

- The Drill is a baboon-like monkey that usually weighs over 50 pounds.

- Drills live in family groups of about 20 or more animals. They are the most endangered monkey here in the rain forest.

- To help save the Drills, governments have made it illegal to hunt them.

Adverbs

Activity One

About Adverbs

An adverb is a word that is used to describe a verb, an adverb, or an adjective. Adverbs tell how, when, or where something happens. *Sometimes* and *quickly* are adverbs in the following sentence: ***Sometimes,*** *I eat* ***quickly*** *when I'm hungry.* As your teacher reads the fact cards about endangered rain forest animals, listen carefully for adverbs.

Adverbs in Context

In a small group, take turns reading each fact card. Make a list of all of the adverbs that you find. Look at the chart below. Sort the adverbs according to whether they describe *how*, *when*, or *where* something happens.

HOW	WHEN	WHERE
quietly	usually	here

Activity Two

Explore Words Together

With a partner, take turns making up sentences about different kinds of animals. Use one or more words from the box on the right to complete each sentence. Talk with your partner about other adverbs you may use.

fast	outside
never	there
often	warmly

Activity Three

Explore Words in Writing

Write a sentence about a rain forest animal without using any adverbs. Trade sentences with a partner. Challenge each other to add adverbs to each other's sentences.

The People of the Rain Forest

by Gail Riley

Imagine that mile after mile of trees where you lived were being cut down and burned every day. Imagine someone knocking on your door and saying, "You're going to have to leave."

Native people who live in the Amazon Rain Forest don't have to imagine these scenes. They experience them every day. More than one fifth of the Amazon Rain Forest has already been destroyed. The forest that remains is in trouble.

Today, the people of the rain forest are battling to save their forests and their way of life. However, there was a time when these people lived in peace with nature.

What mental images do you have in your mind as you read? How do those mental images help you understand what this selection is about?

A Long History

The story of the rain forest people begins long ago, when glaciers covered Asia, North America, and South America. Scientists believe that groups of people traveled from Asia to the Americas across great land bridges. Some of these people settled in the rain forests.

For centuries, the native people carefully used the land. They hunted and gathered only what they needed. Vines swayed, flowers blossomed, and jaguars roared. They lived in harmony within a perfectly balanced ecosystem.

The Balance Is Broken

In the 1500s, Europeans began traveling to the South American rain forests. They brought their way of life from Europe. Unfortunately, they also brought disease to the native peoples. These diseases were devastating for the many rain forest communities.

How do you picture the rain forest before the 1500s? How do you picture the rain forest in the 1800s?

In the 1800s other explorers discovered that the rain forest was filled with trees whose sap was useful in making rubber. Inventors discovered many different ways to use rubber. The demand for the rubber tree sap increased.

Some native peoples moved deeper into the forest. They wanted to avoid contact with those who were coming to tap the rubber trees and export the sap.

The Balance is Still Broken

The damage that began in the 1800s continues today. Agriculture, the cattle industry, and logging all harm the rain forest. In many parts of the forest, the air is filled with the sound of bulldozers and the smell of burning trees. Experts say that if the destruction continues at the same pace, half of the Amazon Rain Forest will soon be gone!

What About the People?

Five hundred years ago, there were an estimated ten million native people living in the Amazon Rain Forest. Today there are probably less than 200,000 native people. Among these surviving people, there are around 200 known native groups.

Each group has its own culture, traditions, and languages. Some native peoples live much like their ancestors did thousands of years ago. Other native peoples live much like we do. One thing they all share, however, is a respect for the forest.

Two-Word Technique Write down two words that reflect your thoughts about each page. Discuss them with your partner.

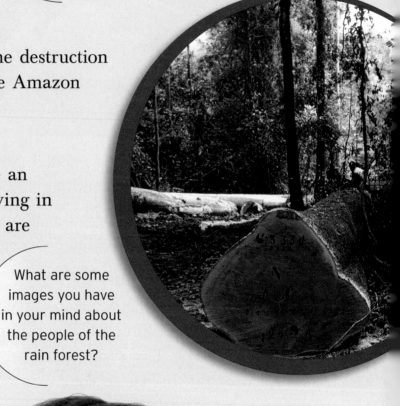

What are some images you have in your mind about the people of the rain forest?

A Culture Survives

The Yanomami (Yah-noh-mah-mee) are a native people who live in the Amazon Rain Forest. There are four major groups of Yanomami. The Yanomami people try to live as they have for hundreds of years. They stay away from outsiders.

Why do you think the Yanomami people want to limit their contact with outsiders?

The Yanomami live in hundreds of small villages throughout the Amazon Rain Forest. In each village, the people live in a large circular building made from vines and leaves. The building has an open-air living space in the middle.

The Yanomami people live in harmony with the forest. One way they do this is called "shifting." They carefully farm in a small area. In each area, a few trees are cut down to let the light reach the forest floor. They burn the trees and put the ashes on top of the soil. The ashes help fertilize the soil. They farm in one place for a few years. Then they move on to another area before the resources are used up.

Although the outside world has tried to change their way of life, they can live entirely from what the rain forest provides them. They show us how the resources of the forest can be used without being destroyed.

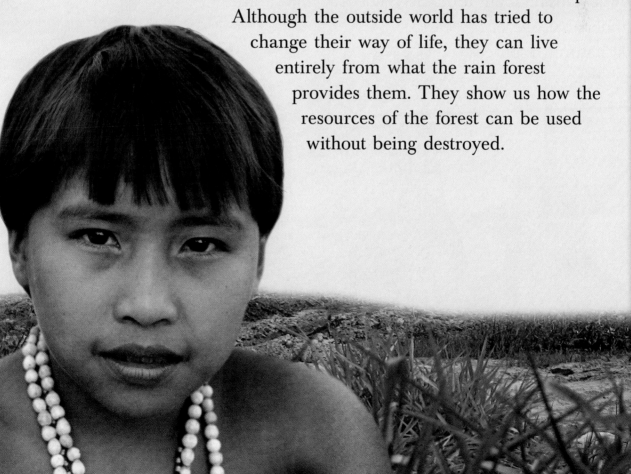

409

Living in Two Worlds

The Yawanawà (Yah-wah-NAH-wah) are another native rain forest people. They lost much of their land and many of their people in the 1800s. They now live on protected Yawanawà rain forest land.

The Yawanawà conduct business in profitable interactions with people that live outside of the rain forest. They sell some of their plants to a cosmetic company. They also make a special rubber that is highly prized.

What mental image do you have of the Yawanawà tribe?

Currently, some of the Yawanawà people are working on a list of rain forest plants. The list contains thousands of years of knowledge about how plants can be used as medicine. At first they wrote all the information on sheets of paper. Now they are working on a computer database. The Yawanawà chief has a computer. It runs on solar power and is connected to a satellite dish.

The Yawanawà can point out a plant in the rain forest that can be used for medicine. Then they can point and click on a website about a disease. The Yawanawà are a reminder that one of the earth's greatest natural resources is its people.

Think and Respond

Reflect and Write

• You and your partner read *The People of the Rain Forest*. Discuss the two words that you wrote.

• Choose two words. On one side of an index card, write the word. On the other side of the card, write the image that the word suggests.

Adverbs in Context

Search through *The People of the Rain Forest* to find adverbs. Make a list of the adverbs you find. Tell which word each adverb describes.

Turn and Talk

CREATE IMAGES: ENHANCE UNDERSTANDING

Discuss with a partner what you have learned about creating images to improve understanding.

• How does creating mental images help you understand what you read?

Think about the mental images you created when you read *The People of the Rain Forest*. Talk about your mental images with a partner. Be sure to use details to explain your mental images.

Critical Thinking

With a partner, brainstorm what you know about the rain forest and the people that live there. Write down your ideas in the left column of a sheet of paper. Look back at *The People of the Rain Forest*. Write down on the right side of the piece of paper what you learned about the rain forest from your reading. Then answer these questions.

• Why do you think the Yanomami do not want contact with the outside world?

• Why do you think the Yawanawà cooperate with the outside world?

• How does the world outside the rain forest help the Yawanawà? How does the work of the Yawanawà help the world outside the rain forest?

So You Want to Help?

You may have learned many new facts about **tropical** rain forests. You may have learned they are in danger, but what can you do? If you try to follow these steps, we might see a big **improvement** in the future of our tropical rain forests. Your actions can change the world!

• **Learn More!** Learn all about the rain forest. Do research to understand the **relationship** between rain forest plants and animals. Find out how the **interaction** between people and the rain forest can be harmful.

• **Spread the Word!** Share what you know with family, friends, and classmates. When people understand the rain forest **ecosystem**, they are more willing to preserve it.

• **Get Write To It!** Find organizations that make donations to sponsor plants and animals. Write to local businesses. Ask them to sponsor a plant, an animal, or things such as "monkey bridges." The bridges allow monkeys to cross over roads safely.

• **Call the Media!** Have your class contact the local media. You can write letters to newspaper editors that inform the community about rain forests. Call a local television station. It might be interested in covering something you're planning, such as a fundraiser or special project.

interaction ecosystem tropical improvement relationship

Structured Vocabulary Discussion

When your teacher says a vocabulary word, you and a partner should each write down the first words you think of on a piece of paper. When your teacher says, "Stop," exchange papers with your partner and explain the words on your lists to each other. Then compare your words with another partner team.

Throughout the week, add to your vocabulary journal entries. Record new insights and other words that relate to this week's vocabulary.

Picture It

Copy this chart into your vocabulary journal. Write words that describe a **tropical** place.

tropical	rainy

Copy this chart into your vocabulary journal. Write words to explain what things might have an established **relationship** with each other in the rain forest.

relationship
plants and animals

Help the Rain Forest!

Save the Earth!

GORILLAS IN THE WILD

by Becky Manfredini

Deep in the rain forest, a tropical one,

Giants roam beneath the hot sun.

A strong silverback leads the way.

He keeps his troop safe from any attack.

He decides when to travel and where they should go.

He gathers his troop. They move to and fro.

Each day when they travel, they find plants to eat—

Fruits, leaves, stems, and seeds are their treat.

Their long arms and hands help them move all around.

They "knuckle walk" over the warm and wet ground.

They love to take naps when it's time for a rest.

Leaves, twigs, and branches are used for a nest.

In the overgrown forest, these giants will talk.

They roar, growl, and chatter. They grunt as they walk.

The troop is a family—a peaceful one,

As they live in the forest, beneath the hot sun.

Grammar

The Rain Forest

Providing for the World

What do bananas, asthma medicine, and basketballs all have in common? They are all made from plants originally found in the rain forest. It may surprise you to find out how many products come from the rain forest.

Foods

Many delicious foods were first found in the rain forest! Do you eat any of these rain forest foods?

bananas	chewing gum	vanilla	spices (ginger, nutmeg)
pineapples	cocoa	rice	
nuts (cashews, macadamia)			

Medicine

Many medicines have ingredients that come from the rain forest. There may be many more medicines we have not yet discovered. Diseases can be treated using medicines made from rain forest plants.

asthma	leukemia	malaria	bronchitis
pneumonia	heart disease	certain kinds of cancer	

Products

The sap from rain forest trees is used to make rubber. Can you add to the list of products that use rubber?

balls	erasers	balloons	tires
garden hose	gym mats		

Prepositions

Activity One

About Prepositions

A preposition shows the relation of a noun or pronoun to another word in a sentence. Many prepositions give more information about the place or motion of a noun or pronoun. Some give more information about time. *Above* and *after* are prepositions in the following sentence: *I looked **above** the trees **after** I heard the macaw's cry.* As you teacher reads *The Rain Forest*, listen carefully for prepositions.

Prepositions in Context

Read *The Rain Forest* with a partner. Then list all of the prepositions that you find. Think of other prepositions you know and add them to your list.

Activity Two

Explore Words Together

In a small group, take turns making up sentences with prepositions, but leave the prepositions out. Exchange sentences with another group and fill in the missing prepositions.

near	through
around	beside
toward	behind

Activity Three

Explore Words in Writing

Write sentences to describe what you learned about products that come from the rain forest. Include as many prepositions as you can. Exchange sentences with a partner. Find and circle the prepositions in each other's sentences.

The FOREST Has EYES

by Joy Nolan

"Don't stray too far from the camp, Tim," Dad warned. "Just hang by the rest of group. You could get lost . . . or eaten."

"By what—*bugs*?" I said, in a tone I knew was kind of bratty. My parents were about to travel deeper into the rain forest than I could go. Well, deeper than they thought I could go! I could have handled it.

He met my eye. "Yeah—*insects*. Some insect bites can kill you. There are also scorpions . . . poison-dart frogs . . . jaguars . . . lions."

"Come on, Dad. There aren't any lions in the rain forest."

"Good, son. You're right." He was smiling now—he was a scientist, and he liked that I knew my facts. Then his face became serious again. "It's very easy to get disoriented in the jungle, even when you are familiar with the area. There are trees and vines so thick that you sometimes can't see ten feet ahead—but you'd better believe all the animals can see you."

What statements from Tim's father are facts? How do you know?

We'd been deep in Brazil's rain forest for four days. So far I had seen the most amazing plants in the world. I had also seen incredible animals. I hadn't seen a jaguar, though, and I really wanted to. As far as I was concerned, jaguars were the real kings of the jungle. Lions don't even live in jungles!

Almost as if he could read my mind, Dad said, "You really do not want to mess with an animal whose name means *he who kills in one leap.* That's the origin of the word *jaguar,* you know."

"Okay, Dad, I get your point!"

He grabbed his gear, and headed off through the trees. I walked back toward the camp. Mom and Dad are medical researchers. They travel all over the world looking for plants that can cure or treat diseases. On this project, they were working with some of the native people to discover some plants that would yield an improvement in medicine.

My family and the rest of the research group were staying at a small camp in the middle of nowhere. You could walk right out the front door and into the rain forest. There was a path crawling with tangled vines, slithering pythons, giant rodents, and insects the size of my hand.

> What are some of Tim's opinions? How do you think his opinions will affect his actions?

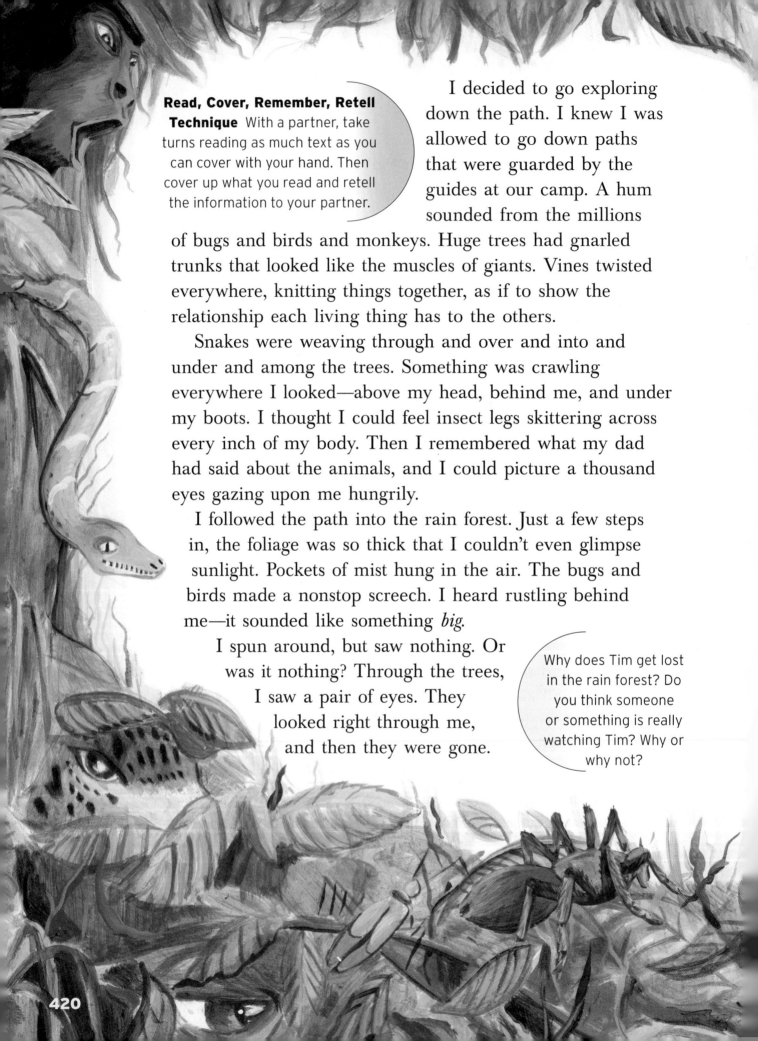

Read, Cover, Remember, Retell Technique With a partner, take turns reading as much text as you can cover with your hand. Then cover up what you read and retell the information to your partner.

I decided to go exploring down the path. I knew I was allowed to go down paths that were guarded by the guides at our camp. A hum sounded from the millions of bugs and birds and monkeys. Huge trees had gnarled trunks that looked like the muscles of giants. Vines twisted everywhere, knitting things together, as if to show the relationship each living thing has to the others.

Snakes were weaving through and over and into and under and among the trees. Something was crawling everywhere I looked—above my head, behind me, and under my boots. I thought I could feel insect legs skittering across every inch of my body. Then I remembered what my dad had said about the animals, and I could picture a thousand eyes gazing upon me hungrily.

I followed the path into the rain forest. Just a few steps in, the foliage was so thick that I couldn't even glimpse sunlight. Pockets of mist hung in the air. The bugs and birds made a nonstop screech. I heard rustling behind me—it sounded like something *big*.

I spun around, but saw nothing. Or was it nothing? Through the trees, I saw a pair of eyes. They looked right through me, and then they were gone.

Why does Tim get lost in the rain forest? Do you think someone or something is really watching Tim? Why or why not?

I started picturing jaguars padding between the trees, poisonous snakes, tarantulas, and scorpions—their tails held high and ready to strike.

I kept creeping along. The sense of possibility of exploring was strong. In just one more step, I knew I'd see something so incredible it would be worth my fear. Then I saw them again—the eyes. They were unblinking and following my every move.

I sprinted away. The jungle got darker and the eyes were closer. I lost my balance and fell into a bush. Ants! They scrambled around me, moving like wildfire. Now I had to turn back—but which way was *back*? The foliage was so thick that I stumbled, over and over. The jaws of the jungle were swallowing me whole.

What facts about the rain forest do you learn from the description of Tim's walk?

I grabbed onto a tree trunk and withdrew my hands in terror. They were covered in a sticky liquid. Was the forest itself trying to capture me? Had there been a victim before me?

A sloth mother and baby hung upside-down in front of me. I ducked under them; they didn't even move. They seemed so calm and peaceful. Would I make it back alive? Only the eyes knew.

There was more rustling—closer, this time. I saw a flash of golden-brown through the leaves. Then I saw them once more—the eyes. They stared at me steadily.

I tried to run. Immediately my legs got tangled in a vine. Something burst through the bushes next to me. I had no time to get away. Curled into a ball, I shut my eyes tight. Something was breathing right over me. I forced myself to open my eyes.

It was a boy about my age. He must have been a member of the Yanomami. He stared at me. He didn't seem unfriendly—just *totally* serious.

I didn't know what to do, but he did. He held out a hand and helped me up. Then he pulled back some vines and pointed. I could see our camp. Strangely, I had not gotten farther than a hundred yards. I let out a sigh of relief, and he smiled.

I waved to my unexpected guide and headed back to the camp. I had some scrapes and bruises, but I'd learned a lesson.

When my parents got back, I was reading.

"Hi, Tim," Mom said. "Want to go out exploring?"

"Nah, that's okay, Mom. I just want to take it easy today."

Has Tim's opinion about the rain forest changed? Why or why not?

Think and Respond

Reflect and Write

• You and your partner have read *The Forest Has Eyes* and retold sections to each other. Discuss with your partner your retellings.

• Choose one fact and one opinion from the story. On one side of an index card list one fact or one opinion. On the other side of the card explain what makes you know what is a fact and what is an opinion.

Prepositions in Context

Search through *The Forest Has Eyes* for prepositions and make a list. Then write sentences about the rain forest. Use at least one preposition in each sentence. Exchange your sentences with a partner and circle all the prepositions in each other's sentences.

Turn and Talk

INFER: FACT/OPINION

Discuss with a partner what you have learned so far about facts and opinions.

• Why is it important to know the difference between a fact and an opinion?

• How does identifying the facts and opinions help you make inferences in your reading?

Discuss with your partner some of the facts and opinions you have from the selection. Talk about how you use facts and opinions in making inferences in *The Forest Has Eyes*.

Critical Thinking

In a small group, brainstorm facts you already know about rain forests. Write your facts on a sheet of paper. Then look back at *The Forest Has Eyes*. Write down the parts of the story that are most probably facts. Then discuss and answer the following questions.

• In reading the story did you learn any new facts about the rain forest? Explain your answer.

• What else did you learn about the rain forest from Tim's experience? Is the additional knowledge fact or opinion? Explain your answer.

In a business letter, an author writes to a business in order to request information, share an opinion, or offer a service. In this letter, Beto writes to learn more about the efforts a riverboat cruise line is making to protect life in the Amazon rain forest.

March 10, 2012

Ms. Albea Montanez

EcoCruise

P. O. Box 5432

San Diego, CA 92126

> The writer begins the letter with the date and the address of the company.

Dear Ms. Montanez,

    I am writing because my class is learning about threats to the Amazon rain forest. I had read that logging was a threat. However, I just learned that tourism can be a real problem, too!

> The writer introduces the topic of the business letter and explains why he is writing.

    I read that your company offers eco-friendly riverboat cruises on the Amazon River. I hope to learn more about your company. I'd also like to thank you for being a leader in helping to change the way that riverboats operate! People should be able to see the Amazon without negatively affecting the plants and animals.

Ms. Albea Montanez
EcoCruise
P. O. Box 54

During class, we talked about the ways that Amazon River cruises pollute the river. Riverboats can produce harmful chemicals, wastewater, and trash. Noise from riverboats can scare animals. I was quite surprised to learn how much damage one boat can do.

The writer provides details that support the topic of the letter.

I read that your boats dispose of waste carefully. You treat and filter wastewater. You also educate guests about how to dispose of their trash properly. I like that you run your engines more slowly when you're near river dolphins. Doing this reduces pollution and noise. These steps can help to protect a fragile environment like the rain forest.

I would like to tell my class more about your company. Please send me more information about how your company is eliminating waste and pollution. Your efforts to protect the environment will encourage other companies to work harder to reduce their pollution. Thank you for caring about the future of the Amazon rain forest.

The writer restates why he is writing and thanks the person reading the letter.

Sincerely,

Beto Delgado

Beto Delgado

Respond in Writing

Answer these questions about the letter you just read.

- What is the main idea of the business letter? How does the writer support the main idea? Provide two or three examples from the letter.

- How does the writer tie the letter together at the end? Include an example from the letter.

Writing: Letter

Use the steps of the writing process to create a letter.
The following tips can help you make your writing its best.

Prewriting

- Choose a person or organization you would like to write to.

- Look up the name of the person you will write to and the address of the place you will be sending your letter.

- Decide on a topic and make a list of the points you want to include in your letter.

Drafting

- Write the body of your letter first. Don't worry about the format while drafting your letter.

- Be clear about why you are writing. Include only points that support the main idea of your letter.

- Think about your audience while writing your letter. Determine whether your letter should have a formal or informal tone.

Revising

- Read your letter to make sure your message is clear. If it isn't, add supporting details to improve your letter.

- Make sure your voice and tone are appropriate for your audience (the person or people who will receive your letter).

- Check that your letter includes the correct date, a person's name with a business address, a salutation, a body, and a closing.

Editing

- Check your spacing, punctuation, and capitalization to make sure your business letter is in the correct format.

- Check that you have placed commas correctly in dates and addresses.

- Make sure you have used adverbs and comparative adverbs correctly.

- Exchange letters with a partner and read each other's work for grammatical, spelling, and formatting errors.

Publishing

- Create a clean final copy of your letter.

- Address an envelope, add a stamp, and drop your letter in the mail.

Market Day at Hojbro Plads, Copenhagen, undated
Paul Fischer (1860–1934)

Viewing

This painting shows an outdoor marketplace in Copenhagen, Denmark. It was painted around 1900, before there were large, indoor supermarkets. Then, people gathered in an outdoor space to buy and sell food, flowers, and other products.

1. What time of day do you think it is in the scene shown by the painting? What else can you tell about the setting of this marketplace?

2. What kinds of activities do you see in the painting? Do they remind you of anything that you have experienced before?

3. Look at the two young girls in the center of the painting. How are these two girls alike? How do you think these girls are different? What clues in the painting show you these differences and similarities?

4. What is your favorite detail in this painting?

In This UNIT

In this unit you will learn how people earn and spend money on goods and services and how to be a smart shopper.

Products and Profits

Contents

A BAND OF ANGELS

by Deborah Hopkinson
illustrated by Raul Colon

Precise Listening

Precise listening means listening to understand characters. Listen to the focus questions your teacher will read to you.

TIMES HAVE CHANGED!

What do you do when your favorite shirt is old and **shabby**? You go to a store to buy another one! In the 1860s, when the Fisk School chorus was traveling around the United States, getting new clothes was not so easy.

In the 1860s people made most of their own clothes. High prices **discouraged** many people from buying ready-made clothes. Some wove cloth at home. Others bought the **material** from a store. Then it would take many hours to make a new shirt!

It's easier to get a **product** today than it used to be. Today, people can shop at malls with many stores. Shoppers can walk from one store to another to find a **fair** price. People can also shop without ever leaving home. They can use the Internet or get catalogs in the mail. After looking at the different shirt styles online or in a catalog, shoppers might call or send in an order. The new shirt is then delivered right to their home.

SALE

DRESSES • SKIRTS • SF

fair discouraged product shabby material

Structured Vocabulary Discussion

Work with a partner to write a word that matches each phrase. When you're finished share your answers with the class.

• *not making progress on a soccer team*

• *a run-down house with weeds in the front yard*

• *two people get the same reward for doing the same work*

Throughout the week, add to your vocabulary journal entries. Record new insights and other words that relate to this week's vocabulary.

Picture It

Copy these charts into your vocabulary journal. First, write the name of a **product** you use in the left chart. Later, in the right chart, list any **material** used to make each product named in the left chart.

Product	Material
shoes	rubber, cloth

Fix-Up Strategies

Read On

When you read a selection, you may come across a word or idea you do not understand. When this happens, think about what the word or idea means. Then read on to look for clues to help you understand.

When you READ ON, you skip a difficult word and read past it.

When you come to a word or idea you do not understand, read on and use the text that follows to help you figure out the meaning.

TURN AND TALK Listen to your teacher read the following lines from *A Band of Angels*. With a partner read the lines from the story. Then, discuss with your partner any words you don't understand. Read the passage and talk about what you learned from reading on.

• Read the first sentence. What do you think *trudged* means?

• Now read on. Look for clues about *trudged*. Was your idea correct? What does the word mean?

"As they traveled from town to town, those nine young singers faced many hardships," Aunt Beth tells me. "Often they were turned away from restaurants because their skin was black.

"One stormy evening no hotel would take them in. They trudged through the rain, until at last someone let them stay in a leaky shed. Ella slept wrapped in her coat, trying to keep warm."

TAKE IT WITH YOU When you read on to figure out the meaning of a word or idea, think like a detective. First decide what you think the word or idea means. Then look for clues to find out if you are correct. Use a chart like the one below to help.

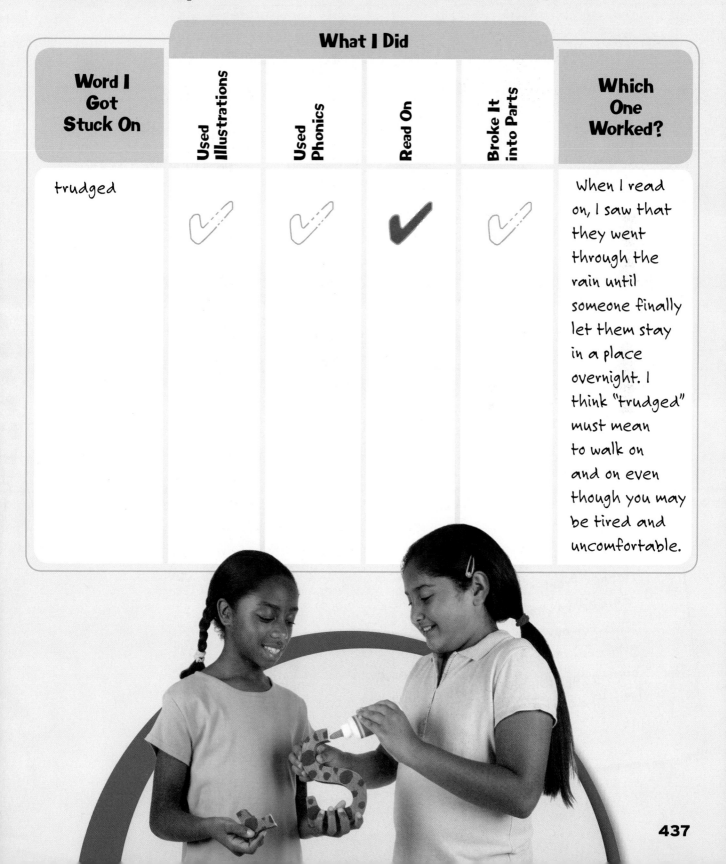

Word I Got Stuck On	What I Did				Which One Worked?
	Used Illustrations	Used Phonics	Read On	Broke It into Parts	
trudged	✓	✓	✔	✓	When I read on, I saw that they went through the rain until someone finally let them stay in a place overnight. I think "trudged" must mean to walk on and on even though you may be tired and uncomfortable.

LEMONS AGAINST CANCER

75¢   75¢

by Theodore Greenberg

April 3 - Today our teacher, Mr. Tanaka, told us about our next class project. We'll sell lemonade at the School Fair on May 12th! The money we make will go to an organization that supports kids with cancer. Because I'm the class secretary, I'll keep a journal of our lemonade stand. I will also figure out how much money we make selling our product.

April 7 - Today we assigned everyone a task for our lemonade stand. Some students will ask local businesses to donate materials for the project. Others will advertise for the stand. Everyone else will help make and sell lemonade.

April 14 - Today we received a letter from a store in town. They agreed to donate lemons and cups for our stand! We are very grateful. The less money we spend buying supplies, the more we will have left to donate to kids with cancer.

April 21 - The School Fair is only three weeks away! Today our class made a list of the supplies we need. Thanks to the donations from stores in town, we only need to buy sugar and ice.

Eva, Jan, Malika, and Ann sell lemonade.

April 25 - Today we painted a sign for the lemonade stand. We decided 75¢ per cup was a fair price to charge. We also sent an ad to our town's newspaper. They will print our ad free because we're working for a good cause. A local radio station is also going to announce our lemonade stand! Everyone in town will know what we are doing.

May 12 - Today was the big day! We set up our table early and waited. We brought four big coolers of lemonade and a box to collect money. At first the weather was cool, so not many people wanted cold lemonade. In the afternoon it warmed up, though. Then we sold a lot! Both students and adults bought the lemonade. I made a graph to show our sales through the day.

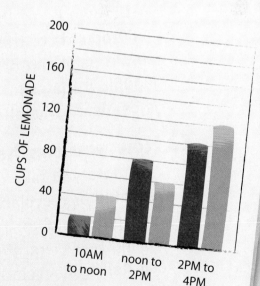

After the fair I counted our money twice. I did not want to be careless with the money. We made $315! We paid $45 for the sugar and ice. So we had $270 to donate. Our class was proud of what we had done.

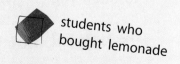
students who bought lemonade

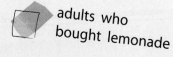
adults who bought lemonade

Got boxes, bottles, bags?
Don't just throw them in the trash can.

CALL Rolling Recyclers!

♲ Who are we?

Rolling Recyclers is a recycling service. Our trucks come to your house and pick up old newspapers, cans, bottles, and more. We make your old items into new, useful materials. Our prices are the best in town!

♲ Why recycle?

Did you know that the average U.S. citizen creates 1600 pounds of trash per year? Every time you throw an old paint can or cereal box into the trash, it goes to a landfill. It may sit in the landfill for years and years. This is careless, wasteful, and harmful to our environment.

♲ How you can help?

Before you take out your trash, remove items that are reusable or recyclable. Wash the items. If they are made of paper, metal, or plastic and you cannot reuse them, call Rolling Recyclers. We will come pick them up. Each time you call Rolling Recyclers, you can feel good that you are helping to save the environment.

Be helpful, not helpless. Have a heart and do your part!

Suffixes -ful, -able, and -less

Activity One

About Suffixes -ful, -able, and -less

A suffix is a word part that can be added to the end of the root word to change its meaning. Use suffixes to help you understand the meaning of unknown words. As your teacher reads the advertisement about recycling, listen for words containing the suffixes -ful, -able, and -less.

Suffixes -ful, -able, -less in Context

Read the ad with a partner. Find all of the words that contain the suffixes -ful, -able, and -less. Make a chart like the one below. Write each word and its meaning. Then list the root word and the suffix in each word.

WORD	MEANING	ROOT WORD	SUFFIX
recyclable	something that can be changed so it can be used again	recycle	-able

Activity Two

Explore Words Together

With a small group, add the suffix -ful, -able, or -less to each word in the box at right. List the new words and look up the meaning of each in the dictionary.

depend	reason
enjoy	care
hope	law

Activity Three

Explore Words in Writing

Choose three words with the suffix -ful, -able, or -less from page 440. Write an advertisement using these words. Share your ad with a partner.

The Shoemaker's Surprise

by Julia LoFaso

SCENE 1: Henry's Workshop

(A shoe store stands in a line of stores.
An old man sits on a workbench inside.)

NARRATOR: For many years, Henry made shoes and sold them from his little shop in the center of town. He created his shoes by hand from the best leather and the finest cloth. Henry's shoes looked great and lasted a long time, but lately he hadn't had any customers. He feared he might have to close his store forever.

HENRY: Business has been slow since the big shoe store opened across the street. We haven't had a new customer in a whole week!

> What does Henry mean when he says that "business has been slow"?

JUNE: Don't worry. People will come back, it's just a slow time of year.

HENRY: I don't know. I went into the big store yesterday, and their shoes are so cheap! However, those shoes will fall apart after six months of wear.

JUNE: We'll think of a way to bring in more customers. Mia and Lucy are meeting us here soon, so let's close up the shop.

HENRY: It's no use being here if no one is coming in.

Characters

NARRATOR

HENRY, a shoemaker

JUNE, his wife

MIA, their nine-year-old granddaughter

LUCY, their ten-year-old granddaughter

SCENE 2: Henry and June's House

(Lucy, Henry, Mia, and June sit at the dinner table eating. Henry can't stop yawning.)

LUCY: Grandpa, you have yawned seven times in a row! Did you get up early?

HENRY: Actually, your grandmother and I have been staying up every night trying to create a new kind of shoe. We need a brilliant idea to save our business, but so far we haven't had any luck.

> What does "brilliant" mean? If you aren't sure, how could you find out?

JUNE: I had high hopes for my spectacular sticky sandals. I thought they would help people stick to the wall like flies, but the sandals always stuck to the floor first!

MIA: I don't understand, Grandpa. The shoes you make are the best around. They last forever and they're so comfortable! Why won't people buy them?

HENRY: Well, Shoemart has a wider variety to choose from than we do. I think they get a new shipment every day. Also, their shoes are so cheap.

LUCY: Oh, I understand! Since Shoemart opened across the street, you have competition. You can't sell your shoes at a lower price, so you want to invent a shoe they don't sell. Then people might be willing to spend more money.

HENRY: Yes, that's exactly right!

MIA: Well don't worry, Grandpa, I'm sure you'll think of something.

SCENE 3: Henry's Workshop

NARRATOR: As soon as Henry arrived at his workshop the next morning, he saw a handwritten note on his workbench.

HENRY: *(picks up the note and starts to read)* "Dear Mr. Shoemaker . . ." *(calls to his wife)* June, you're not going to believe this!

Reverse Think-Aloud Technique Listen as your partner reads part of the text aloud. Choose a point in the text to stop your partner and ask what he or she is thinking about the text at that moment. Then switch roles with your partner.

JUNE: *(reading aloud over his shoulder)* "We have a genius idea for a new shoe called the Spring-o-matic Super Sneaker. It will help kids jump to unbelievable heights when they play basketball. We created these plans, but we don't have the tools needed to make the shoes ourselves. Can you help? Yours Truly, The Elves."

HENRY: Elves? Are there really elves? Well, I guess it doesn't matter—this idea is from a genius! The shoes even have a special stopping device to help you land on your feet. They are astonishing!

What does Henry say that helps you understand what "genius" means?

JUNE: *(laughs)* I'm certain those sneakers would sell really well. If I were a little younger, I'd buy them myself! I think you should try it.

HENRY: I definitely will. I don't have any orders to fill right now, so I might as well try to make a pair, especially since the design is right here.

SCENE 4: Henry's Workshop

(Henry walks into the workshop carrying three huge bags.)

NARRATOR: Henry got to work right away. First he went to purchase all the materials he would need. Then he set to work to make the Spring-o-matic Super Sneakers.

JUNE: *(watches Henry)* What is that?

HENRY: *(takes items out of the bag)* I bought leather and cloth from the fabric store and sturdy metal springs from the hardware store.

JUNE: *(looks confused)* Springs?

HENRY: The plans call for me to build them into the bottom of the shoe. *(points to the shoe plants)* See, the note says right here: "The Spring-o-matic Super Sneaker uses springs to give you upward motion when you jump." The only problem is that the springs were expensive. These sneakers will have to be more expensive than the sneakers at Shoemart if I want to make a profit.

What do you think the word "profit" means here? What clues tell you so?

JUNE: Oh, people won't mind paying extra for shoes this unusual. I guess there really are elves!

NARRATOR: Henry soon completed a pair of Spring-o-matic Super Sneakers. The shoes were an instant hit! Henry and June were thankful they had many customers again. Henry wanted to share their new wealth with the elves, but they were nowhere to be found.

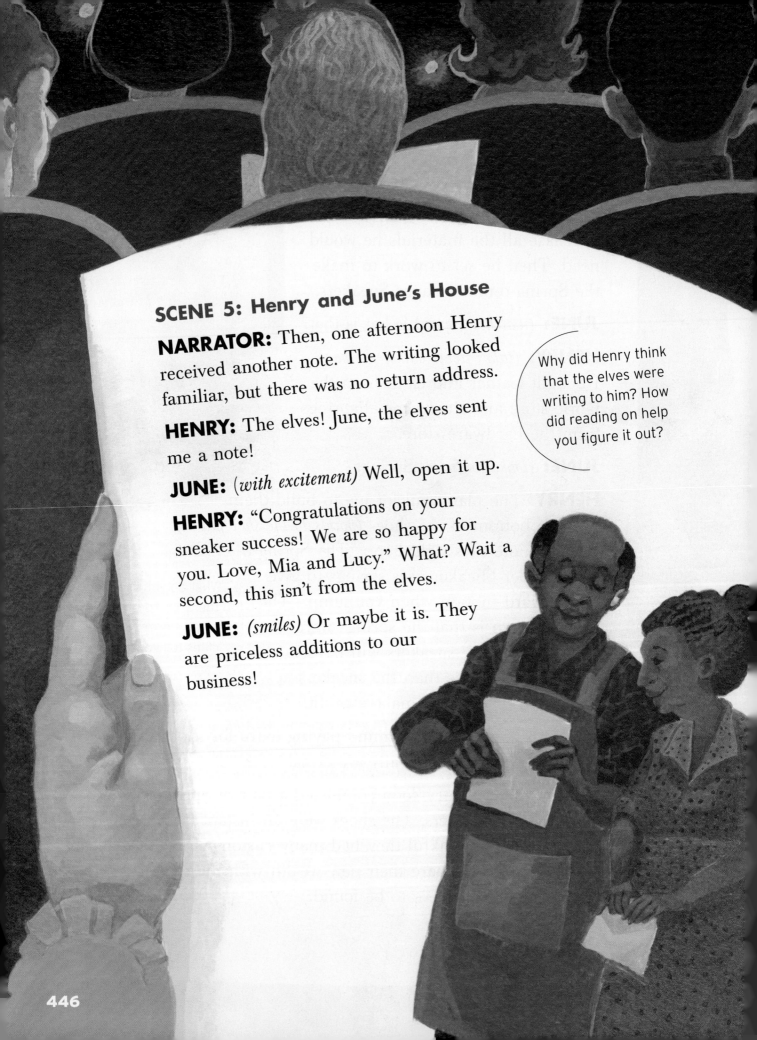

SCENE 5: Henry and June's House

NARRATOR: Then, one afternoon Henry received another note. The writing looked familiar, but there was no return address.

HENRY: The elves! June, the elves sent me a note!

JUNE: *(with excitement)* Well, open it up.

HENRY: "Congratulations on your sneaker success! We are so happy for you. Love, Mia and Lucy." What? Wait a second, this isn't from the elves.

JUNE: *(smiles)* Or maybe it is. They are priceless additions to our business!

Why did Henry think that the elves were writing to him? How did reading on help you figure it out?

Think and Respond

Reflect and Write

- You and your partner have read *The Shoemaker's Surprise* and asked questions about what you were thinking. Discuss words that were difficult to understand and your strategy for understanding them.

- Choose two of the words from your discussion. On one side of an index card write the word. On the other side of the card write the word's meaning.

Suffixes *-ful*, *-able*, and *-less* in Context

Many different words share the same suffixes. Some of these suffixes are *-ful*, *-able*, and *-less*. Search through *The Shoemaker's Surprise* to find some of these suffixes. List the words you find and discuss them with a partner. How does the suffix help you understand each word's meaning?

Turn and Talk

USE FIX-UP STRATEGIES: READ ON

Discuss with a partner what you have learned so far about reading on to help you understand what you are reading.

- What does it mean to read on?

- How can reading on help you to understand difficult words or ideas?

Think about words or ideas from the play that confused you at first but made sense later. Write down a few examples. Compare your examples with those of a partner.

Critical Thinking

With a partner, write a list of the things that sellers have to think about when setting the price of their product. Write your ideas down on a sheet of paper. Then look back at *The Shoemaker's Surprise*. Write a list of the things Henry had to think about in selling his shoes. Then, answer these questions:

- How does a big shoe store decide on the price of its product?

- How is this process different from how Henry set his prices?

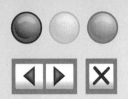

www.KidCoinCollector

Do you want to start a coin collection? Maybe you want to add to your collection. Find out how at Kid Coin Collector! Follow these bulleted links for more information:

- **Collector Stories** Where do kids get the **inspiration** to take up this fun hobby? How do they find their coins? Read about kids just like you who own hundreds of coins.

- **Coin History** This page contains a **wealth** of facts about coins. There are more facts about coin history here than on any other Web site. For example, did you know that people made coins in China 3,000 years ago? Find out more!

- **Buying, Selling, and Trading Coins** Perhaps you want to trade coins with another collector. Read tips on how to **negotiate** a fair trade with that person. Perhaps you want to sell a coin that is worth a lot of money. Learn how to make a **profit** by selling the coin for more than you paid for it.

- **Discussion Board** Here you can talk to others about your collection. You can also **advertise** events that collectors might want to attend. Don't worry, this is a safe discussion board for kids only!

Thanks for visiting Kid Coin Collector!

Structured Vocabulary Discussion

When your teacher says a vocabulary word, you and your partner should each write down the first words you think of on a piece of paper. When your teacher says, "Stop," exchange papers with your partner and explain any of the words on your lists to each other.

Throughout the week, add to your vocabulary journal entries. Record new insights and other words that relate to this week's vocabulary.

Picture It

Copy this chart into your vocabulary journal. Add words with meanings that are similar to **negotiate**.

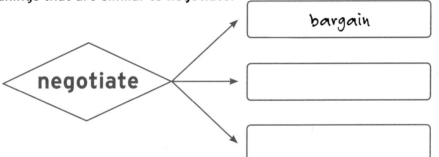

negotiate → bargain

....

Copy this idea wheel into your vocabulary journal. Fill it in with places where people **advertise**.

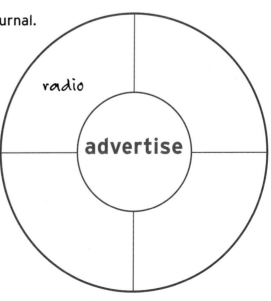

radio / advertise

449

A DAY FOR A DOLLAR

by Becky Manfredini

I'm fresh off the press from a money machine.

I'm new to this world, I'm crispy and green!

First I'm shipped to a bank and put in a pile

Where I wait with excitement for the longest while.

Finally I'm picked up and given away

By a woman who takes me to the world's best café.

She hands me over for a cup of hot tea.

Where will I go next? What will happen to me?

I'm put in a drawer but get yanked out again
to make up the change for a neat, crispy ten!
Then I'm stuffed in a pocket, exhausted and worn
Where I'll nap forever. At least I'm not torn!

I start to wake up as I float to the ground.
My owner just lost me. I don't make a sound!
I'm found by two kids as I wait all alone.
I'm so glad I'm no longer out here on my own!

They talk and negotiate on how to spend me.
What amazing toy will they buy? They just can't agree.
So instead they will save me and put me away.
Thank goodness—it's been an unbelievable day!

From a Tree to your Table

1. Oranges are grown in warm, sunny places like Florida and Texas. When the fruit is ripe, workers pick it and put it into sacks.

2. Workers then move the oranges to large 900-pound tubs. The tubs are put onto a truck and taken to a production plant, or factory.

3. At the factory, oranges are checked for freshness, roundness, and juiciness. Machines squeeze the juice from the best oranges. Then the juice is poured into cardboard cartons, or glass or plastic jugs.

4. A cold truck takes the cartons to a store.

5. You and your family can then buy the fresh juice at the store for your enjoyment. Drink all the orange juice you want to your satisfaction.

Suffixes *-ness*, *-ion*, *-tion*, and *-ment*

Activity One

About Suffixes *-ness*, *-ion*, *-tion*, and *-ment*

A suffix is a word part that can be added to the end of a root word to change its meaning. Use suffixes to help you understand the meaning of unknown words. Adding suffixes will change the spelling of some root words. Your teacher will read the article called *From a Tree to Your Table*. Listen carefully for words containing the suffixes *-ness*, *-ion*, *-tion*, and *-ment*.

Suffixes *-ness*, *-ion*, *-tion*, and *-ment* in Context

In a small group, read the article together. List all of the words that contain the suffixes *-ness*, *-ion*, *-tion*, and *-ment*. Put your words in a chart like this.

WORD	MEANING	ROOT WORD	SUFFIX
freshness	like new	fresh	ness

Activity Two

Explore Words Together

With a partner, add the suffix *-ness*, *-ion*, *-tion*, or *-ment* to each word at right. List the words. Then take turns using each word in a sentence.

helpful	observe
effective	measure
reduce	excite

Activity Three

Explore Words in Writing

Choose three words with the suffix *-ness*, *-ion*, *-tion*, or *-ment* from page 452. Write a short article using these words. Tell about how a product you like is made or sold.

A Family Affair

by Will Otero

Many people dream of owning a business someday. Just a few years ago I was one of those people! I loved to cook. I was good with money, too. So I dreamed of opening a small restaurant or café. I wanted my café to be a place where everyone was welcome like part of the family. What I didn't know was how much work it would take to make my dream come true. I also had no idea how many people would help me along the way!

How important was Will's dream to him? What makes you think so?

I have loved food since I was a little boy. I grew up with six brothers and sisters. My mom was a single mother so she had to work very, very hard to take care of us! But we were never hungry.

She made delicious *sancocho*. *Sancocho* is a Puerto Rican stew made from many vegetables. Sometimes she sent me to the *bodega*, or corner store, to get food for our meals. She was friendly with the family that owned the store, so they always gave us what we needed. I remember feeling such a strong sense of love and belonging when I went to that store.

When I got older, I worked on farms during school breaks. My brothers and sisters and I went to the country to pick cucumbers, tomatoes, or watermelons to earn extra money for the family. I really didn't want to work while other kids enjoyed their time off. I complained and complained. But I learned how to work hard during those vacations!

Nothing is more tiring than working in the hot sun hour after hour. Now I'm so glad to have a job I love.

I worked as a waiter in restaurants as I got older. Once I took a job at a famous amusement park. A friend found me a job there as a "prep cook," getting ingredients ready for other chefs to use.

What mental images help you understand how Will feels about his mother's cooking?

Say Something Technique Take turns reading a section of text, covering it up, and then saying something about it to your partner. You may say any thought or idea that the text brings to your mind.

Soon I became a "line cook," putting each meal on its plate before it is served. I loved working in kitchens, so I decided to go to cooking school!

Later, when I knew I wanted to open my own business, I took many jobs to earn money. I worked in a bank, and that's when I learned about investing money, which is one way to make money grow over time. I learned about loans, when people borrow money from a bank. And I learned about debt, which means you owe money. The most important thing I learned about debt is that I don't want to have any!

Why do you think Will says he doesn't want to have debt?

I knew I would need lots of money to start a business. So one day I took a big risk. I invested all the money I had saved. I gave it to a friend I trusted. To my amazement, he helped me double my savings!

Other people helped me with their kindness, too. When I had finally saved enough to open the café, many people pitched in! My brother helped find wood and other things I needed to build the inside of the café.

We went to secondhand stores and bought materials at great prices. One friend painted beautiful pictures on the café walls. Another friend made the lights out of metal. Still another friend did the dangerous work to put electric wiring in the café. Even Mom helped by breaking down old walls with a hammer! She really is my business partner and my inspiration. With so many good people like my mom helping, I knew the café would be successful.

Our café has not been open for very long, but already it is earning money. That is important, because many businesses do not earn money for a long time. One reason we are successful is that I am a great cook! I bake all our cookies, muffins, and breads myself. Restaurants all over San Francisco buy them to serve to their own customers. I like to think you can taste my love for the café when you eat my cooking.

Another reason people come here is that we are part of the community. There are many people in our neighborhood who have little money. We keep prices low so they can eat here.

How do you think Will feels about his mom? What clues help you to know this?

457

We also help groups in the neighborhood by donating food and time. For example, we have hosted several dinners with a Puerto Rican culture theme. People pay to enter, and Mom cooks an incredible feast including sancocho, rice and beans, bread pudding, and more. Then a live band comes to play salsa music, and everybody dances! We use the money to send local senior citizens to art classes.

Look back at the description of Will's party with a Puerto Rican theme. What pictures do you get in your head as you read?

We do not advertise for these dinners. People just hear about our cooking and come from all around. I also think they come because ours is a place to eat, laugh, and have a good time as if you were family. As my mom says, your family is made up of all the people who love and support you. I think she is right, because so many people have helped to make my dream come true.

Think and Respond

Reflect and Write

• As you read *A Family Affair*, you and your partner shared your thoughts and ideas. Discuss these thoughts and ideas with your partner.

• On one side of an index card write the clues from the passage that helped you form the mental image you have of Will and his family. On the other side of the index card write your mental image.

Suffixes *-ness, -ion, -tion,* and *-ment* in Context

Search through *A Family Affair* for words with suffixes *-ness, -ion, -tion,* or *-ment*. Discuss what each word means and how the suffix helped you figure it out. Then write a paragraph about taking a trip to a store. Use the words in your paragraph.

Turn and Talk

CREATE IMAGES: ENHANCE UNDERSTANDING

Discuss with a partner what you have learned so far about creating mental images to help your understanding of text.

• What does it mean to create mental images as you read?

• How do mental images help you better understand a selection?

Discuss with your partner a mental image you have of Will Otero and his family and how that mental image helped you understand his story better.

Critical Thinking

In a small group, discuss the challenges that go with owning a small business. Write a list of the challenges on a piece of paper. Then return to *A Family Affair*. Make a list of the challenges Will faced when opening his café. Then, answer these questions.

• How are Will's challenges like those of other small business people you have read about? Explain your answers.

• Do you think Will can be a successful owner of a small business?

In a personal narrative, an author writes about an event that happened in his or her own life. In this personal narrative, Marco writes about a fun run he helped organize.

Movin' Shoes
by Marco Donato

Last month, my class learned that there are students in Africa who don't have shoes. Our teacher, Mr. Lomong, also told us about an organization that helps. They send new and lightly used shoes to Africa. Right then, all of the kids in my class knew they wanted to help. We decided to organize a fun run in our community!

To get our charity event started, each student signed up for a job. Some students wanted to design a running course around the park. Others would make posters to advertise the run. Volunteers would also contact companies to request donations. I signed up as the organizer!

> The writer clearly introduces the main idea of the personal narrative.

> The writer links ideas using transition words and phrases.

Next, we voted on a name for our fun run. My class decided to call our event "Movin' Shoes for Africa." I thought it was the perfect name! We used the name to decorate posters and flyers.

> The writer uses time-order words to sequence events in the order that they happened.

Finally, I came up with a great idea to charge a special admission fee to the run. Each person would need to donate one lightly used pair of shoes! I didn't think people would mind parting with their old shoes to help such a wonderful cause.

The day of the run was amazing! People came from all over the city to participate. We collected over 100 pairs of new and lightly used shoes. I know those shoes will make a big difference for students in Africa.

I'm really glad that I helped to plan "Movin' Shoes for Africa." I learned a lot about working with others and helping out in my community.

> The writer concludes by reflecting on his experiences.

Respond in Writing

Answer these questions about the personal narrative you just read.

- How does the writer organize events in this personal narrative? What words and phrases help you understand the order of events?

- How does the writer feel about the event his class is planning? Explain how the writer's use of voice and punctuation helps you to know how he feels. Use details from the personal narrative to support your answer.

Writing: Personal Narrative

Use the steps of the writing process to create your own personal narrative. The following tips can help you make your writing its best.

Prewriting

- Make a list of important or exciting events from your life. Then choose one event to write about.

- List what you saw, heard, smelled, tasted, and touched as part of this event or experience.

- Think about how this event or experience made you feel from beginning to end. List your emotions.

Drafting

- Use dialogue, interesting facts, and action words to grab your reader's attention.

- Consult your prewriting often to make sure you are including the important details about your event or experience.

- Describe what you learned or how you changed as a result of this experience.

Revising

- Check that your events are written in the order that they happened.
- Show your work to a partner and ask if anything looks confusing or out of place.
- Eliminate details that do not add anything to your purpose for writing.
- Let your personality shine through in your writing by carefully choosing your words and punctuation.

Dictionary

Editing

- Check that you used prepositions correctly and placed prepositional phrases appropriately.
- Check that all titles and proper nouns are capitalized.
- Look at your work several times, reading for a different issue each time. For example, check punctuation first, correct capitalization issues on the next reading, and look for spelling errors on the following pass.

Publishing

- Choose a strong title to interest your reader.
- Make a clean copy of your personal narrative. Illustrate or include photos of key events.
- Post your personal narrative online for others to read.

Buying Smart

Contents

BOSS OF THE PLAINS

THE HAT THAT WON THE WEST

by
Laurie Carlson

pictures by
Holly Meade

Strategic Listening

Strategic listening means listening to make sure you understand the story. Listen to the focus questions your teacher will read to you.

A HOT Idea for Cold Weather

Kathryn "K-K" Gregory
Kid Inventor

Harsh weather inspired the broad **brim** of the Stetson hat. Severe weather also inspired a young girl to invent a new product to protect her wrists from the cold.

The idea was born on a frosty day in 1994. Ten-year old Kathryn "K-K" Gregory was trying to build a snow fort, but the snow kept creeping between her mittens and coat sleeves. So what did K-K do? She invented fleece cuffs to protect her wrists.

First K-K gave her friends samples of her invention. They were a hit! People began to **suggest** that K-K sell her product. K-K applied for a patent and started her own company. Her invention began to **impress** people, and the **demand** for her product grew. A television ad sold more than 2,000 pairs in six minutes. The invention also won awards. News stories about the business began to spread.

Being a kid and a business owner was not easy. It was hard for K-K to juggle school and her booming business. At first K-K's company struggled to make a big enough **supply** for the demand. However, K-K's business is still a successful company today. She no longer works there, but she still follows the progress of the company she started.

Structured Vocabulary Discussion

Work with a partner or in a small group to fill in the following blanks so that the first pair of words has the same relationship as the second pair of words. When you're finished, share your answers with the class. Be sure you can explain how the words are connected.

Throughout the week, add to your vocabulary journal entries. Record new insights and other words that relate to this week's vocabulary.

• *Baseball cap* is to *bill* as *cowboy hat* is to _____.

• *Discover* is to *invent* as *amaze* is to _____.

• *Struggle* is to *attempt* as *hint* is to _____.

Picture It

Copy this word organizer into your vocabulary journal. Fill in the circles with examples of things that may **impress** people.

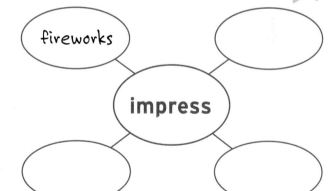

Copy this chart into your vocabulary journal. Write a sentence that tells why there is a **demand** for a product you list.

Demand
The telephone helps people communicate.

Synthesize
Classify and Categorize Information

When you classify and categorize, you identify words or concepts that share similar characteristics. You then can put the words or concepts into groups based on the similar characteristics. Organizing information in this way helps you understand how the information relates to what you already know.

To **CLASSIFY** and **CATEGORIZE** means to group things that are the same.

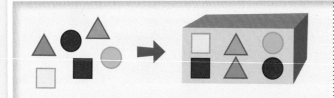 As you read, sort ideas and information into groups.

TURN AND TALK Listen to your teacher read the following lines from *Boss of the Plains*. With a partner, discuss ways to organize and group the important information. As you work with your partner, answer these questions.

• Which facts or ideas in this passage have something in common?

• How can these groups help me understand the passage?

John Stetson was determined to succeed. He remembered the horseman out West who had thought that his high-crowned, wide-brimmed hat was just right. Maybe other Westerners would like it too—bullwhackers, who drove oxen; mule skinners, who led mule teams; and drovers, who herded cattle or sheep. He'd make a hat for the wranglers and cowboys of the West. And he knew just what he'd name his new hat: Boss of the Plains.

TAKE IT WITH YOU Classifying and categorizing can
help you understand how things are related in meaning. This
process will help you put together, or synthesize, information
from what you read. As you read other selections, use a
chart like the one below to help you classify information.

	People who might wear a Stetson	Kinds of hats people wore
Categories		

	People who might wear a Stetson		Kinds of hats people wore	
Examples	bullwhackers	wranglers	knit caps	calico sunbonnets
	mule skinners	cowboys	wool derbies	homburgs
	drovers		straw sombreros	slouch hats
			army hats	silk high hats

Sunday at the FARMERS' MARKET

by Sarah Hughes

Generations side by side
Selling treats from far and wide
All at the farmers' market.

Loudly and clearly vendors yell
Asking buyers to touch and smell
All at the farmers' market.

Potatoes, plums, and pumpkins, too,
Piping hot bread and vegetable stew
All at the farmers' market.

Find carrots fresh, and berries ripe,
As for lettuce, there's every type
All at the farmers' market.

Families arrive from near and far
Some on foot and some by car
All at the farmers' market.

They'll buy flowers in every shade
Homemade muffins and lemonade
All at the farmers' market.

Your hard-earned money can buy a lot
Try some cider—delightfully hot
All at the farmers' market.

The crowds are coming, better get there soon
The best of it will be gone by noon
It's Sunday at the farmers' market!

Greetings from Bangkok!

Dear Tanya,

We've been in Thailand for a week now. The best part has been meeting our Thai relatives. They greeted us joyfully as we got off the plane, and we felt like we had known them forever. My cousin Nhing and I are almost exactly alike. Of course she's very cool.

Yesterday we went to the Damnoen Saduak Floating Market. It is called the floating market because there are hundreds of small boats selling their goods. We had to get up very early because later in the day the market gets crowded with tourists. We hired a boat to get around. We had to step in slowly and carefully. I didn't want to fall in the water!

We could buy all kinds of fruits and vegetables. They had straw hats, carved wooden statues, and amazing silk dresses. We compared prices before we bought anything. I found out I'm good at bargaining. I paid 210 baht (Thai money) for a dress that would normally cost 500 baht! You may think that's still a lot, but 210 baht is about 5 U.S. dollars!

I'll go back to the market tomorrow, and see if I can find another bargain for you. See you soon!

Your friend,

Mali

Suffixes -*ly* and -*fully*

Activity One

About Suffixes -*ly* and -*fully*

You can use what you know about suffixes to help you understand the meaning of a new word. Adding the suffix -*ly* adds the meaning "in a way that is" and -*fully* adds the meaning "in a way that is full of." As your teacher reads Mali's letter, listen for words with the suffixes -*ly* and -*fully*.

Suffixes -*ly* and -*fully* in Context

With a small group, read the letter and make a list of all the words you can find with the suffixes -*ly* and -*fully*. Make a chart like the one below. Write each suffix and root word. Then write the whole word and its meaning.

ROOT WORD	SUFFIX	WORD	MEANING
joy	fully	joyfully	in a way that is full of joy

Activity Two

Explore Words Together

Work with a partner to add the prefix -*ly* or -*fully* to each of the words on the right to make new words. Be ready to share the new words and their meanings with the class.

quick	hope
cheer	fear
clear	quiet

Activity Three

Explore Words in Writing

Write a postcard to a friend using at least three words with the suffixes -ly and -fully. Then share your postcard with a partner. Have your partner find and circle the words you used that have the suffixes -*ly* and -*fully*.

Buy! Buy! Why?

By Gail Riley

Did you get a good look at that ice cream on the TV commercial? Yum! Wouldn't it just melt in your mouth?

Truthfully, the ice cream would not taste very good. It was probably vegetable shortening mixed with corn syrup, powdered sugar, and flavorings. Shortening is actually a fat used to prepare food. It's not something you want to eat!

What about the sizzling burger in the next commercial? It looks delicious, right? Chances are, the burger was propped up with cardboard and smeared with petroleum jelly to make it shiny. Then extra sesame seeds were glued to its bun. A mouthful of cardboard and glue doesn't sound too appetizing either, does it?

Food advertisers don't usually use plain old products in their commercials. They hire "food stylists" to dress up a sandwich as if it is a supermodel! When you learn to recognize these and other advertising tricks, you can make yourself a smart buyer. Let's take a peek inside the world of advertising. It will make you think twice before you purchase your next item!

> What do food advertisers have in common?

Yum!

Delicious?

Fake!

476

You've Got the Power!

Did you know you have buying power? People who advertise products call your age group Tweens. That's a nickname for preteens and young teens. Advertisers have learned that Tweens are big spenders! Your opinions are very important to companies. They want to make sure you think what they're selling is cool.

Companies want you to buy food, electronics, toys, and other items. They want to get your hard-earned allowance and babysitting dollars. They try to reach you in many ways, including TV, movies, video games, print ads, and the Internet.

An advertiser thinks that Tweens are easily persuaded. They show their products on television to millions of Tweens at one time. The commercials try to sell the idea to Tweens that their products are so important that Tweens must buy them. Advertisers know that adults have a hard time saying "No," too.

How could you categorize most of the facts on this page?

The Truth About
TWEENS

FACT: Tweens are spending at least $11 billion dollars each year! Parents are spending another $176 billion on their Tweens each year.

FACT: Most Tweens watch about 20,000 TV ads each year.

FACT: Almost half of American families with children have a VCR or DVD player, video games, a computer, and a TV.

Take a Close Look!

Think carefully as you watch ads on television. In fact, take a look at a few of the ways companies try to get your business.

Partner Jigsaw Technique
Read a section of the article on advertising with a partner and write down the category you discussed. Be prepared to summarize your section and share the category.

BANDWAGON Everyone else is doing it, so you should do it, too.

Example of an ad: "Two out of three kids think our jeans are the best!"

LOOKS AND PERSONALITY Others will want to spend time with you if you use the product in the ad. They will think you are better looking, smarter, or have a better personality.

Example of an ad: People want to spend time with a fashion model who uses a certain kind of shampoo.

AMAZING PLACES If you use the product, you'll feel as though you're happy in a wonderful place—because that's what you see in the ad.

Example of an ad: Family members sip cold orange juice on a sunny beach.

WORDS THAT EXPRESS STRONG FEELINGS The ad includes words like *bold, clever, fearless, daring, lucky, fantastic, joyful*. These words make you think of the product when you think of a time you had these feelings.

Example of an ad: "I feel fantastic when I drink this brand!"

CELEBRITY BRANDING Famous people recommend or use the product in the ad.

Example of an ad: A famous pop star or athlete wears a hat or carries a bag with the advertiser's logo or name.

What other examples of ads that fit into one of these categories have you seen?

478

It's Right in Front of You!

Have you ever noticed how many minutes of ads you see in one TV program? An hour-long TV show sometimes has as many as 19 minutes of commercials!

TV isn't the only place advertisers place ads to reach you. Ads shout from the radio. They jump out at you from billboards. They're waiting on Internet pages and in movies. Sometimes, they're even hiding in the video games you play.

Imagine you're racing a car down the track in a video game. You screech around a corner and just miss running into a billboard—a billboard for a fast food restaurant. You speedily make it to the finish line. Flags wave to show that you finished in first place. The flags show the logo of a popular running shoe. These are examples of "silent ads."

Silent ads can creep into places where you're not watching for them. They might also stick in your memory and pop into your mind when you least expect them to appear.

**TV Show:
41 Minutes**

**Ads:
19 Minutes**

**TV Show Time
vs. Ad Time**

How could you classify the information on this page?

Make Your Voice Heard!

If you disagree with the way a product is advertised, here's what you can do. Don't compromise your beliefs. Write letters and emails, or make phone calls to make your voice heard.

SOUND OFF!

You can contact:
- the television or radio station that aired the ad
- the company that makes the product
- the company that makes a video game or game system with "silent ads"
- people who represent your state in Congress

TOUCH THAT DIAL

For a full day, turn off your TV and radio. Don't visit Internet sites or play video games that include "silent ads." Encourage friends, family members, and others in your school and community to do the same on this special day. Let advertisers and TV and radio stations know why and when you plan to do this.

TUNE OUT

Turn down the volume each time an ad runs on TV or the radio. Fast-forward through commercials if you have video recorded a show.

BECOME AWARE

Talk to friends and family members about what you see and hear in ads. Read magazine articles and books about smart buying. Check out Web sites that are created to keep consumers like you aware of what they're buying.

What do all the ideas on this page have in common?

Think and Respond

Reflect and Write

- You have read a section of *Buy, Buy, Why?* Discuss with your partner the categories you decided on and the information that falls into each category.

- Work with your partner to write the names of your categories on an index card. Then on the other side write important information about each category. Then find a set of partners who read different sections and compare categories.

Suffixes *-ly* and *-fully* in Context

Search through *Buy! Buy! Why?* to find words with the suffixes *-ly* and *-fully*. List each word and circle its suffix. Use what you know about the meaning of the root word and the suffix to write each word's meaning.

Turn and Talk

SYNTHESIZE: CLASSIFY/CATEGORIZE INFORMATION

In small groups discuss why classifying and categorizing the information in a selection helps you to better understand what you read.

- What do you do to classify and categorize information from a selection?

- How does this help you understand what you read.

Think about the categories of information you discovered in *Buy, Buy, Why?* Talk about those categories with a partner.

Critical Thinking

In a small group, look back through *Buy, Buy, Why?* List methods that advertisers use to convince Tweens to buy their products. Then discuss these questions.

- What ads have you seen that use advertising tricks?

- Where do you notice the most advertising—magazines, television, radio, Internet, video games, films? Explain your answer.

- Do such advertising tricks work for you? Why or why not?

What's the Best Toothpaste Around?

Your local toothpaste **merchant** will absolutely **recommend** PERFECT PASTE!

Why does it cost a bit more than other leading brands?

PERFECT PASTE contains special ingredients that actually straighten your teeth!

Do you want whiter, brighter, straighter teeth?

Purchase PERFECT PASTE. Use it for a month.

You'll agree that it is a **bargain**!

Don't **compromise** when it comes to your smile!

BEFORE PERFECT PASTE

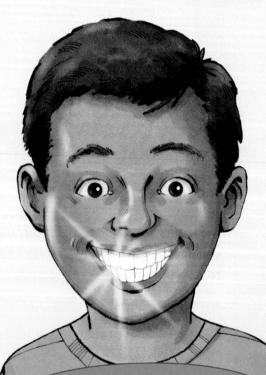

AFTER PERFECT PASTE

Structured Vocabulary Discussion

Work with a partner to review your new vocabulary words. Then classify the words into one or two categories of words: words that describe something you can do, and words that describe someone or something.

Throughout the week, add to your vocabulary journal entries. Record new insights and other words that relate to this week's vocabulary.

SOMETHING YOU CAN DO	SOMEONE OR SOMETHING
recommend	bargain

Picture It

Draw a web like this in your vocabulary journal. Fill in the circles with words that describe a **bargain**.

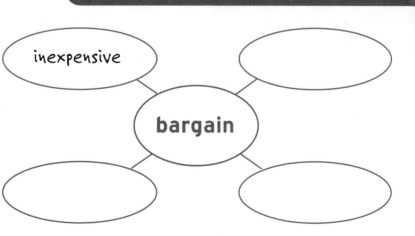

inexpensive

bargain

Draw a chart like this one in your vocabulary journal. Fill in this chart with items you have bought that you would **recommend** and items you would not **recommend**.

Recommend	Do Not Recommend
mystery novel	musical toothbrush

In the 1800's, merchants often sold their goods in the street from carts. To encourage people to purchase their goods, they often sang catchy tunes. Sometimes, merchants even included jokes in their songs to get buyers' attention.

HOT CROSS BUNS

Traditional

Hot cross buns!

One-a-penny buns!

One-a-penny,

Two-a-penny,

Hot cross buns.

If you have no daughters,

Give them to your sons!

One-a-penny,

Two-a-penny,

Hot cross buns!

PAPERBOY'S SONG

Traditional

Headlines! Headlines!

Get the latest news here.

Tonight people everywhere will sleep

to ring in a New Year!

Headlines! Headlines!

Read all about it.

Defeated candidate tells country:

"I quit!"

Headlines! Headlines!

You heard it here first.

The Sun's the best newspaper,

The Post is the worst!

Let's Get Down to Business

Have you ever thought about starting a business? To begin, you need a good idea for what you will sell. One of the key ingredients to any successful business is selling something that other people want!

A business can either sell items or a service. For example, you could sell items, such as jewelry or crafts that you made. A business can also provide a service that others need, such as babysitting or dog walking. When you have your idea, you'll need to follow some steps in order to make your business a success.

First, you'll need to make a business plan. In this plan, you set goals and do research to see if there's a market for what you're selling. Your idea might seem great, but it won't work if people won't buy. Then there's the price. It will need to be high enough to make a profit for you, yet low enough to be fair.

You'll need some money to get started so you'll have to earn or borrow that. Also, once you get going, you'll need to keep good records. You will need to keep track of the cost of your supplies. You will also keep track of the profits. Starting a business is a lot of work, but it can be fun, too.

Conjunctions

Activity One

About Conjunctions

A conjunction is a word that connects words, or groups of words, or sentences. Some conjunctions—*and, but, or, nor, for, so,* and *yet*—join parts of a sentence. Some conjunctions come in pairs, such as *either/or* and *both/and*. Some conjunctions, such as *when, however, that,* and *what* join two clauses to make a complex sentence. As your teacher reads *Let's Get Down to Business!* listen carefully for conjunctions.

Conjunctions in Context

With a partner make a list of conjuctions you remember from the article. Then read the article together and add any new conjunctions to your list. How many conjunctions were you able to find altogether?

Activity Two

Explore Words Together

and	that
either	but
or	yet

Look at the conjunctions listed on the right. Work with a partner to think of sentences using these conjunctions. Discuss how the conjunctions connect words or parts of sentences together. Be ready to share your sentences with the rest of the class.

Activity Three

Explore Words in Writing

Imagine that you are starting a business. Write a TV or magazine ad for the product or service you will be selling. Use as many conjunctions as you can in your ad. Share your ad with a partner.

The Two Merchants

retold by Julia LoFaso   **A Folktale From Uganda**

A long time ago, a man named Akello lived with his wife Miremba. They lived near a large lake that sparkled in the sun, and banana trees surrounded their home. The trees gave them shade. The lake gave them water.

> Look at the word *surrounded*. Read on to find clues about its meaning. What do you think *surrounded* means?

Akello was a merchant. Every weekend, he went to the market to sell packages of fried ants. Early one morning, Akello was getting his packages ready to sell. First, he gathered ants. Then, he took off their wings and put the wings in a pile to throw away. Akello was wrapping the ants in banana leaves when suddenly he got an idea.

"If I wrap the ant wings," he thought, "Someone will purchase those, too."

Akello smiled and rubbed his hands together. "People will think they're getting a package of delicious ants to eat," he thought, "No one will know."

Just then, Miremba walked into the room. Her arms were full of banana leaves. She looked at Akello's package of ant wings and frowned.

"What do you think you're doing?" she asked Akello. "No one eats ant wings! They taste awful."

"Don't worry," he said. "This little trick I'm going to play will make me rich by the end of the day."

"If you say so," Miremba said, "but it's not fair." Akello did not listen. He put his ants in a sack, and he carried them off to the market.

Across the lake from Akello lived another merchant named Ochen. Ochen lived with his brother in a village full of colorful mango trees. Ochen was a cloth merchant. He sold fine fabrics at the market. Usually, he sorted through his cloth for the best pieces to sell. One morning, Ochen thought of a sneaky plan. He rolled some old rags into a bundle and wrapped the bundle in a beautiful piece of fine cloth. Ochen chuckled. "Someone will pay a lot for this," he thought.

Ochen's brother walked into the room with water from the lake. "Why are you wrapping rags?" he asked, "No one will want to buy those."

What is "sneaky" about Ochen's plan? How is it like Akello's plan?

489

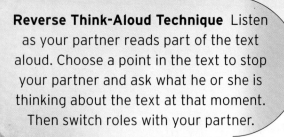

Reverse Think-Aloud Technique Listen as your partner reads part of the text aloud. Choose a point in the text to stop your partner and ask what he or she is thinking about the text at that moment. Then switch roles with your partner.

"No one will know," Ochen said, "This little trick I'm going to play will make me rich by the end of the day." Ochen's brother shook his head, but he didn't say a word. Ochen packed his cloth and left for the market.

Ochen walked from the west side of the lake. Akello walked from the east side of the lake. The two merchants arrived at the market as the sun began to rise. They set up tents for shade. All around them, other merchants laid out goods for sale. Akello waited for someone to buy his ant wings, and Ochen waited for someone to buy his bundle of rags. The noisy and bustling market was full of people.

"Fresh fish!" shouted the fish merchant.

"Ripe fruit!" the fruit merchant called.

Children laughed and ran among the different merchants. Their parents carried baskets full of food and clothes.

Describe the market. Find the sentences that appear after the word *market* on this page. How did they help you with your description?

After many hours, it was almost time for the market to close. The customers left for their homes. Some merchants packed up to leave. Ochen still had not sold his bundle of rags. Akello still had not sold his ant wings.

Finally, the sun began to set at the market. Ochen and Akello were the only two merchants left.

Ochen had not eaten since morning. His stomach growled so loudly that Akello heard it and turned around. "You sound hungry," Akello said. He reached for the package of ant wings. "How would you like to buy some tasty ants?"

Think about the trick the merchants are playing. Why does Ochen say that Akello is getting a bargain?

"Well," said Ochen, with a mischievous twinkle in his eye, "I don't have any money, but how about a trade? I can trade you this fine cloth for your ants. It's the most beautiful piece I have," Ochen told Akello, "I'm giving you a pretty good bargain if you ask me."

"OK," Akello answered, "Let's trade."

Akello gave the ant wings to Ochen. Ochen gave the rags to Akello. The two merchants packed up their tents and left. By the time Akello got home, the sky was dark. He told his wife Miremba what happened at the market.

"What a poor fool!" Akello chuckled, "I got this exquisite piece of cloth and he's stuck with a package of ant wings."

Miremba said, "Why don't you open the bundle?" Akello unrolled the piece of fine cloth. Out tumbled a pile of rags.

"That cheat!" Akello shouted, but then he remembered his own trick. He wagged his finger at Miremba and made a promise. "I have no more tricks to play. I'm an honest man as of today."

As soon as Ochen got home, he howled with laughter.

"What a miserable fool!" Ochen crowed to his brother. "I got this gigantic package of ants and all he got was a measly bundle of rags."

"Why don't you open the ants?" Ochen's brother said.

So Ochen unwrapped the banana leaves, but all he found inside was a pile of ant wings.

"That liar!" Ochen cried, but then he remembered what he had done to Akello. Ochen told his brother, "That was the last trick I'll ever play. I'm an honest man as of today."

From that day on, Akello and Ochen sold only their finest goods at the market.

Akello is angry and calls Ochen a "cheat." Then his feelings change. How do you know? Which sentences tell you this?

Think and Respond

Reflect and Write

- You and your partner have taken turns reading *The Two Merchants*. Discuss the questions and answers and choose two words or passages about which you had questions.

- On one side of an index card, write the word or passage. On the other side, tell what you learned by reading on.

Conjunctions in Context

A conjunction is a word that joins two parts of a sentence. The words *and*, *but*, *as*, *so*, *that*, *because*, *when*, and *while* are all conjunctions. Search through *The Two Merchants* to find as many conjunctions as you can.

Turn and Talk

FIX UP STRATEGIES: READ ON

Discuss with a partner fix up strategies you can use when you do not understand a part of a story.

- What does the strategy "to read on" mean?

- How can reading on help you understand a part you just read?

Look back at the first two paragraphs on page 488. Talk with a partner about how reading on helped you understand this part of the story.

Critical Thinking

With a partner, discuss what makes a good bargain when you are buying and selling goods. Review the events in *The Two Merchants*. Write a sentence or two describing how Ochen and Akello planned to trick their customers. Then answer these questions.

- Did the two merchants make good bargains with each other? Why or why not?

- Were the two merchants smart buyers or sellers? Why or why not?

- What do you think the experience of Ochen and Akello can teach you about buying and selling goods?

In a poem, an author uses rhythm, rhyme, imagery, and strong details to describe a subject and relate his or her feelings about it. The subject can be a person, place, event, or other topic. In this poem, Jasmine writes about the life of a veterinarian—a job she hopes to have one day.

The Happy, Hard Life
of a Veterinarian
by Jasmine Hodges

The sun blazes down and my hands are sticky.

I'm helping a horse in a field's muddy dirt.

I try not to mind all the heat and the filth,

A vet only cares about how animals hurt.

> The writer uses descriptive words and starts the poem with a vivid image.

I live way, way out on a ranch in the country,

Where daily I journey from farm to farm.

I pack a handful of tasty treats in my pocket.

I carry a heavy medicine bag on my arm.

I take out my tweezers to aid a small puppy.

He has a sharp thorn stuck in his wagging tail.

I give a few shots to a sheep with a cold.

I bandage a cow who has tripped on a rail.

> The writer introduces and describes the narrator early in the poem.

Whether the animals are sick or in pain,

They trust me to put them back on the mend.

They don't scamper away or tremble in fear.

They know I'll help them feel better again.

> The writer uses strong verbs to describe the action.

One curious part about being a vet

Is that I long for a day when nobody calls.

That would mean all the creatures are healthy

In their pastures, pens, prairies, and stalls.

Hopefully that wonderful day will arrive.

Until then, I'll work and keep making my rounds.

It's the best employment I could ever imagine,

No matter how hot or difficult it sounds!

> The writer describes the thoughts and feelings of the narrator.

Respond in Writing

Answer these questions about the poem you just read.

- Poems are often broken into lines and sometimes follow a rhyme pattern. Does this poem use a rhyme pattern? If so, provide examples.

- How does the writer use punctuation and capital letters to help the reader understand the poem? Find examples and describe how they help make the writing clear.

Writing: Poem

Use the steps of the writing process to create your own poem.
The following tips can help you make your writing its best.

Prewriting

- Brainstorm and make a list of possible topics for your poem.

- Make a list of your feelings about each topic. You should feel strongly about the topic you choose.

- Think about the five senses as you gather details about your topic.

Drafting

- Focus on your feelings and write what comes to mind.

- Play around with different words to see which ones create the right feeling.

- Try mixing sensory details together to create vivid images.

- If you get stuck, consider how a rhyme scheme might help you finish your poem.

Revising

- Check to see if changes to your line breaks will make your poem more interesting or easier to read.

- Use a thesaurus and dictionary to find words that have the precise meaning you need.

- Replace ordinary words with more specific ones.

- Read your poem to a friend to get suggestions for improving your work.

Editing

- Look for conjunctions in your poem and make sure you are using them correctly.

- Highlight relative adverbs and make sure you are using them appropriately.

- Track your most frequent errors. Keep your own checklist, and refer to it during editing.

Publishing

- Select a strong title to engage your reader.

- Illustrate your poem by adding a drawing or photograph.

- Consider posting your poem online for others to read.

Glass Windows, Bahamas, 1885
Winslow Homer (1836-1910)

THEME **15** Earth Long Ago

THEME **16** Wearing Away

Viewing

This painting shows Glass Window Bridge, a real rock formation that connects two pieces of an island in the Bahamas. Under the natural bridge, the gray, choppy waters of the Atlantic Ocean crash into the clear and calm waters of the Caribbean Sea.

1. Why do you think this rock formation was named the Glass Window Bridge?

2. Why do you think the artist chose to paint this scene?

3. What do you think the artist would have seen if he had painted these rocks thousands of years ago?

4. What might have caused changes to Glass Window Bridge between then and when this painting was created?

In This UNIT

In this unit you will read about Earth's land and living things from long ago. You will also read about how the earth can change over time.

Contents

Dinosaur Tree

by Douglas Henderson

Critical Listening

Critical listening means listening to compare and contrast ideas in the passage. Listen to the focus questions your teacher will read to you.

A Living FOSSIL

One day in 1938, a fisherman off the coast of South Africa pulled up his net. He didn't know it at the time, but that net held a prehistoric fish! Marjorie Courtney-Latimer came to look at the catch when the boat pulled into shore. She worked at a local museum.

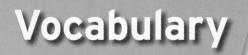

Marjorie opened the net. She picked through fish and slime. Then she saw a fish. It was about five feet long. It had blue-gray scales and strange fins. Marjorie wrote to L. B. Smith. He was also a scientist. Marjorie wanted him to **examine** the fish carefully. He found **evidence** that it was a coelacanth (SEE-la-kanth). This was an amazing discovery. Coelacanths were supposed to be extinct!

Scientists knew about the **fossil** of a coelacanth. Such fossils were 60 million years old. Coelacanths had seemed to **vanish**. Scientists thought they had become extinct with the dinosaurs.

The coelacanth has some unusual characteristics that scientists want to study. Its scales have tiny tooth-like spikes. These spikes protect the fish if it should **scrape** against rocks. The fish lives in caves on the underwater slopes of volcanic islands.

Structured Vocabulary Discussion

Work with a partner to review all of your new vocabulary words. Then classify the words into two categories: words for things and words for actions. When you're finished, share your conclusions with the rest of the class. Be sure you can explain why each item belongs in a category.

Throughout the week, add to your vocabulary journal entries. Record new insights and other words that relate to this week's vocabulary.

Picture It

Draw a chart like this in your vocabulary journal. List words that describe what a **fossil** looks like. Then list kinds of fossils from Earth long ago.

Fossil	
Describe It!	Kinds of Fossils
hard	dinosaur

Copy this word organizer into your vocabulary journal. Fill in the empty circles with things you might want to **examine**.

an animal track

examine

Comprehension Strategy!

Monitor Understanding

Genre

Identifying the genre, or kind of writing, will help you recognize important parts of the text. You can then use your knowledge of genre to understand the text better.

We read different kinds of texts, called **GENRES**, in different ways.

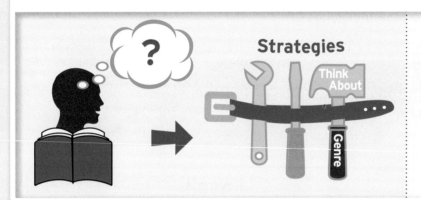

Strategies

Think About

Genre

When you don't understand, think about what you know about the genre to help you.

TURN AND TALK Listen to your teacher read the following lines from *Dinosaur Tree*. With a partner, discuss the genre. Talk about the clues that helped you decide the kind of writing the selection is. Then answer these questions.

- Could the events described in these paragraphs have happened in real life? What makes you think so?

- What clues tell you that the little tree is like a character, instead of a real tree?

The little tree is in danger of being eaten because many plant-eating reptiles roam the stream banks and the quiet, shadowed forest. Once, a small dinosaur, a Revueltosaurus, stopped and looked right at the little tree, then walked on. The little tree just kept on growing, slowly turning air and sunlight into more leaves and roots and woods.

TAKE IT WITH YOU As you read other selections, think about how knowing the genre can help you understand what you are reading. Use a chart like the one below to help you.

Page Where I Noticed I Didn't Understand	What I Did						Which One Worked?
	Reread	Reflected On Purpose	Thought About Meaning	Asked Myself Questions	Thought About Strategies	Used Genre Knowledge	
The page where one small dinosaur stopped and looked at the little tree and then moved on. The text sounds like a story. The little tree is like a character in a story.	✓	✓	✓	✓	✓	✔	I can use my knowledge of a story to understand that this didn't really happen exactly the way that it is told, but that the story is a way to tell about how a tree could become a fossil.

T. Rex Sue Sold to Field Museum

by Gail Riley

Chicago, Illinois–Today the Field Museum introduced Sue to the world. Sue is the most complete Tyrannosaurus rex fossil ever found. From her small, bird-like feet to her large, sharp teeth, Sue is one big fossil! Unlike most dinosaur skeletons you see, Sue is not made of plastic or plaster.

The story of Sue began at a ranch in South Dakota. In 1990, Susan Hendrickson and other fossil hunters were searching the Black Hills for evidence of life long ago. They had found only partial sets of bones. Then one day, they stumbled across a dead horse. They took time to find the owner.

The owner was rancher Maurice Williams. Williams asked the fossil hunters if they would like to examine his land for fossils. During one visit to the ranch, Hendrickson saw a cliff far away. She wondered if the cliff might hold fossil treasures.

Then one day a tire on the fossil hunters' truck went flat. Some of the fossil hunters went to town to get the tire fixed. Hendrickson decided not to go. She decided to try to walk to the cliff instead. At first, thick fog sent her traveling in a circle. When the weather was clear, though, she walked the seven miles to the cliff.

T. rex skull: 5 feet long

T. rex Skeleton: 200 Bones!

At the cliff she found bones that led to the discovery of Sue. It took two years to dig all the bones out of the ground. The assembled bones led to many discoveries, including the theory that dinosaurs are linked to birds. Sue has a wishbone, a special bone found only in today's birds!

After Sue's discovery, there were many legal battles. People could not agree on who owned the fossil because it wasn't clear who owned the land where Sue was found.

Finally, the rancher won the right to make decisions about what should happen to Sue. He sold her to the Field Museum in Chicago. And the rest, as they say, is history!

Entire skeleton: 42 feet long

Foot to Hip bone: 13 feet high

Skeleton weighs 600 pounds!

Laugh-O-Saurus

Mr. Salazar always found interesting, funny ways to teach science. No one was ever bored in his class. Malika and I told him some jokes to add to his collection.

"Mr. Salazar, what do you call a fossil that won't do dishes?" I asked.

"I have no idea," he said.

"Lazy bones!" I said with a giggle.

"Oh!" Mr. Salazar cried. "That's a good one. Do you have any more?"

Malika scrunched up her nose. Then she said, "Aha! I know one. Why did the Archaeopteryx (ar-key-OP-ter-x) catch the worm?" Mr. Salazar said, "I don't have the foggiest idea." "Because it was an early bird!" Malika cried. "Get it?"

"Stop!" I said, laughing uncontrollably at the corny jokes. "What do you call a sleeping T. rex?"

"A dino-snore," Malika snapped back in the blink of an eye.

"Wow!" Mr. Salazar said as he laughed right along with us. "I'll have to share some of these with the class tomorrow. These jokes are really dino-mite!"

Interjections

Activity One

About Interjections

An interjection is a word used to show strong feeling. Usually, an interjection appears alone, is capitalized, and is followed by an exclamation mark. Listen for interjections as your teacher reads *Laugh-o-Saurus* to you.

Interjections in Context

Read *Laugh-o-Saurus* with a partner. Find the interjections and their punctuation. Make a list like the one below to show what you find.

INTERJECTION	PUNCTUATION
Oh	!

Activity Two

Explore Words Together

Have a conversation with a partner about an interesting discovery or a favorite event. Include in your conversation the interjections listed on the right.

Yes!	Wait!
Look!	No!
Super!	Quick!

Activity Three

Explore Words in Writing

Work together as a small group to use interjections from Activities one and two to write a short play about fossil hunting. Include as many interjections as possible in your play, and circle each one. Then perform your play for the class.

THE HATCHLING

by Ann Weil

"Okay, Trevor. We're almost there," Jenny said as she hurried her cousin across the field. Trevor was spending his winter vacation on his aunt and uncle's ranch in Montana. Soon he saw Jenny's twin brother, Jonathan, ahead of them.

"What's going on?" Trevor asked.

"Jonathan thinks there is a maiasaur (MY-a-sar) nest here," Jenny explained. "That's a kind of dinosaur."

Trevor began to recognize a depression in the ground, like the top of a miniature volcano. It looked like Jonathan and Jenny had been hard at work with snow shovels, because they were standing in the only area of the depression not covered in snow.

What type of text are you reading? How can you tell?

"If this is a nest," said Trevor. "It sure is a big one."

Jonathan carefully lifted what looked like a big stone from the frozen dirt. It was about eight inches long with round edges, like a lopsided football.

"Look! This is an egg," said Jonathan. "And I'm going to hatch it."

Jonathan gently carried the egg back to the ranch in a backpack filled with hay and feathers.

"I know I'm not a 'dinosaur hunter' like you, Jon," said Trevor. "But how do you know it's not a fossil? The last live dinosaur hatched from an egg in Canada more than 10 years ago. And that wasn't a maiasaur."

"This is a real egg, I know it!" said Jonathan. "I've been reading about maiasaurs, and the spot where we found this egg would have been perfect for a nest."

Trevor wasn't convinced, but when they got to the barn, they all went to work. Jonathan explained that dinosaurs like the maiasaur might be related to birds. Because the twins' family raised chickens, he figured they could take care of the egg the same way.

Jenny made a soft pile of hay under some heat lamps. Then Jonathan placed the egg in its new nest.

Days passed as the egg sat under the heat lamp. Trevor and the twins checked on it constantly at first, but they had started to lose hope.

Then, on the last day of Trevor's visit, something changed.

How does recognizing the genre help you understand what the characters say?

Say Something Technique Take turns reading the passage aloud with a partner. Cover up a part of the text as you read and say something about it to your partner. You may say any thought or idea that the text brings to mind.

In the morning Jenny noticed a thin crack in the extra-large eggshell. Then the egg started to rock a little.

"Guys, come quick!" she shouted excitedly. "I think the egg is going to fall over!"

Trevor and Jonathan ran over instantly. The egg rocked on, and then they heard what sounded like a tiny claw scratching and scraping the inside of the shell. *Scritch, scratch . . . scritch, scratch . . . scritch, crack!*

"Oh! It's hatching!" Jenny exclaimed with delight.

"Welcome to the 21st Century, Baby!" said Jonathan proudly as the tiny dinosaur emerged from its shell. "I think you need a name."

Could the events on this page happen in real life? Why or why not?

"How about Maya?" Trevor said with a smile.

The creature crawled out of her shell and looked around. She was about a foot long and had a short snout and dark, wide eyes. She looked up at the cousins and blinked. The creature looked so cute that she could hardly be a threat to anyone.

"So, what is a maiasaur exactly? I mean, what do we do with it?" Trevor asked hesitantly. He thought about what a big responsibility it was to take care of such a fragile creature. Everyone got quiet.

Jenny pulled a print-out from a website on maiasaurs out of her pocket. "A maiasaur has a special snout that looks sort of like a duckbill. It is an herbivore, which means it eats only plant foods."

Trevor and Jenny guarded Maya while Jonathan ran to the garden to get a head of lettuce for food.

When he returned, he said, "OK, everyone, let's get chewing! We have to act like the mother maiasaur, and mother maiasaurs chew food for their babies!"

Jonathan popped a few lettuce leaves in his mouth and started chewing. Then he spit the chewed up lettuce leaves into his hand.

"Yuck!" said Trevor. "That's disgusting." Then he looked at Maya, who was hobbling to her feet. "I guess that's what we have to do to help her eat."

Jonathan fed the wet, chewed up lettuce to the baby dinosaur, who gobbled it up.

"Well, you were right about maiasaurs eating plants," Trevor said. "How big is this baby going to get?"

Even though this page has facts, how can you tell it is fiction?

"Well, Trevor, you might be sorry you asked," said Jenny. "My printout says the last maiasaur that hatched in captivity grew to be 30 feet long and weighed 3 tons. Eventually the zoo where it lived had to build a new building just for its food!"

How did identifying the genre of the text help you understand what you read?

Trevor and Jenny looked at baby Maya. What were they going to do?

"I think we should call the Dinosaur Rescue Organization," said Jenny. "They take care of dinosaurs that are too big or dangerous to live with people. Maybe Maya can live on one of their dinosaur preserves."

"Do you really think Maya would be happy on a preserve with all different kinds of dinosaurs, so far from where she was born?" asked Trevor with a frown.

"I think she'd be happier on a preserve than all alone in this barn," said Jenny.

"What are you guys so worried about?" Jonathan called from the entrance to the barn. He walked towards them with a big smile on his face. Then he pulled off his backpack and gently reached in and pulled out another maiasaur egg.

"Hey, Maya!" called Jonathan lovingly. "Get ready to meet your new brother or sister!"

"Oh no! Jonathan, you didn't!" Jenny exclaimed.

"I'll have to come back for a visit really soon," Trevor said laughing. "You guys are going to need all the help you can get!"

Think and Respond

Reflect and Write

- You and your partner have read *The Hatchling* and said something about your thoughts or ideas. Discuss with your partner some of your thoughts and ideas about the story.

- Choose two ideas. On one side of an index card, write a thought or idea. On the other side, explain how the thought or idea helped you understand the story as science fiction.

Interjections in Context

Search through *The Hatchling* to find interjections and make a list. Then use those interjections to write what might happen next in the story.

Turn and Talk

MONITOR UNDERSTANDING: GENRE

Discuss with a partner what you have learned so far about using genre to help you understand the text.

- How did knowing the genre help you better understand the story?

Discuss with a partner the clues that helped you identify the genre for *The Hatchling*. Compare your clues and genre with your partner's.

Critical Thinking

Think about the characters and events in *The Hatchling*. With a partner create two lists of events or facts in the story. The first list is events in the story that are realistic, or based on scientific theories. The second list is events in the story that are fictional. Then answer these questions:

- What events could be true in the story?

- Why do you think a writer would choose to include things that are not realistic? Explain your thinking.

PREHISTORIC AMERICA

Now available on DVD!

"Oh, give me a home, where the mastodons roam, and the saber-toothed tigers can play..."

Does this song sound familiar to you? Would you **recognize** it if the animals were deer and antelope instead of **prehistoric** creatures? *Prehistoric America* is an amazing DVD. It takes viewers on an unforgettable journey to a time in North America 14,000 years ago.

This journey introduces viewers to strange and fierce-looking creatures that no longer exist. Buy this DVD to get the rest of the story! **Review:** ★★★☆

DVD Features!

This amazing DVD includes:

- a question and answer segment with the director.
- a behind the scenes look at the making of the DVD.
- interactive fun facts
- over 20 prehistoric animals to select from and learn what led to their **extinction**.

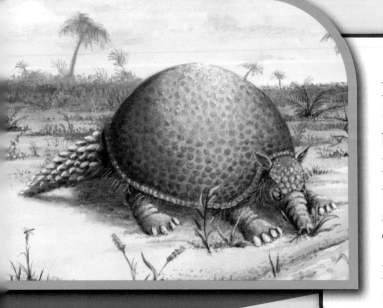

An extinct giant armadillo-like animal called the glyptodon (GLIP-tuh-don) was covered in body armor from head to tail. It was a **threat** to the saber-toothed cat—a huge, ferocious animal with 8-inch-long teeth! The glyptodon would club its prey with its tail as a **method** to capture them.

extinction   recognize   method   prehistoric   threat

Structured Vocabulary Discussion

Work with a partner to match a vocabulary word with each description. Explain the reasons for your choice.

ancient times   *causing harm or pain*

no more dinosaurs

Throughout the week, add to your vocabulary journal entries. Record new insights and other words that relate to this week's vocabulary.

Picture It

Draw a web like this in your vocabulary journal. On the top half of the circle, list reasons that may have lead to the **extinction** of prehistoric animals. On the bottom half of the circle, list animals that are extinct.

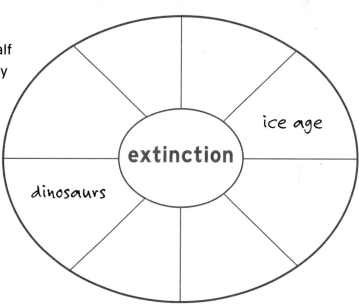

ice age

extinction

dinosaurs

Draw a web like this one in your vocabulary journal. Fill in the boxes with facts about **prehistoric** times.

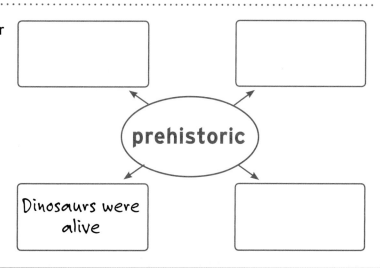

prehistoric

Dinosaurs were alive

519

Ancient Masters of the Earth

by Becky Manfredini

The museum sighs with relief,

as another day passes

with the bones in place.

But the halls whisper, *"Beware!"*

When I see the razor teeth and long tails,

I can imagine the skeletons

scrambling past paintings and roaring at statues.

Do the walls tremble in fear of these beasts?

These powerless bones won't wake up.

They are frozen in a time long, long ago.

But millions and millions of years ago,

these ancient masters of the Earth roamed free.

What did they sound like,
how did they move—
swaying, stomping,
swinging, roaring?

I think up images.
I say their names aloud:
Iguanodon, Stegosaurus,
Triceratops, Apatosaurus.

Their extinction marks an end of an era,
an era filled with these
amazing, ancient masters
who once roamed the Earth.

Incredible Invertebrates!

Think about the last time you took a walk in your backyard. Maybe you saw some small invertebrates such as flies, ants, or earthworms. Now imagine your backyard 300 million years ago. Some of those small, harmless creatures would have been almost as big as you!

Today *millipede*
A millipede is long, fast, and has many legs. You might see a millipede under a rock or between cracks in a sidewalk.

300 Million Years Ago
Long ago, a millipede might have had 30 pairs of legs and been more than 3 feet long.

Today *cockroach*
Maybe you have seen cockroaches. They are insects that can live almost anywhere. Today, a common cockroach might be the size of your thumbnail or as long as your pointer finger.

300 Million Years Ago
Long ago, a cockroach might have grown to be as big as your hand!

Today *dragonfly*
A dragonfly is a flying insect. Like other insects, a dragonfly has no backbone. Instead it has 3 main body parts, plus legs, and long wings.

300 Million Years Ago
Scientists believe that an ancient dragonfly might have had a wingspan as long as your arm!

Compound Words

Activity One

About Compound Words

A compound word is made up of two smaller words combined to make one new word. You can figure out the meaning of a compound word by thinking about what each smaller word means. Listen as your teacher reads *Incredible Invertebrates!* to see if you hear any compound words.

Compound Words in Context

With a small group, look back at *Incredible Invertebrates!* to find compound words. Make a chart like the one below to show what you find. Use a dictionary to check if you are correct about each word's meaning.

COMPOUND WORD	WORD PARTS	WHAT IT MEANS
backyard	back + yard	land behind a house

Activity Two

Explore Words Together

Work with a partner to identify the two words that make up each compound word on the right. Discuss what you think each word means and write your ideas on a sheet of paper.

barefoot   weekend

spotlight   whenever

timeline   brainstorm

Activity Three

Explore Words in Writing

List other compound words you know. Discuss what each means with your partner. Then write a paragraph about Earth long ago using three words from your list.

Nate Murphy and the MYSTERY SAUROPOD

by Julia Wolf and Nate Murphy

Have you ever wondered what it is like to dig for dinosaurs? That's what Nate Murphy does. Nate is a paleontologist, a scientist who studies dinosaurs. He runs the Judith River Dinosaur Institute in Malta, Montana. The Institute has a museum and a summer dig program for anyone over age 14.

Nate made one of his most exciting discoveries on a dig in 2005. But the story really begins around 1986. A rancher found some odd rocks by a hillside on his ranch. He pocketed a few and took them home. For 18 years he did this. One day his daughter saw the rancher empty his pockets. When she asked her father about the odd rocks, he showed her what he had collected over the years. He had 5 buckets of rocks in all!

That is where Nate comes in. Nate looked at the rancher's rocks, and discovered that they were actually the prehistoric bones of a dinosaur. In 2004, Nate and his dinosaur dig teams began excavating at the ranch. But it wasn't until 2005 that it got really exciting.

What did Nate and the rancher have in common?

Here are some of Nate's recollections from a week in the summer of 2005.

Nate Murphy

The team sets up camp.

Day 1

People are flying to Billings, Montana, from all over the country to be part of the Mystery Sauropod Excavation. Soon we'll be driving the 100 miles to the ranch where we set up camp.

I can't wait to get started. I know the bones belonged to a kind of sauropod, but I'm not sure which one. That's the mystery! Maybe it's a sauropod no one has ever discovered before. I can't be sure yet. We have to get down to the digging!

Day 2

We have to clear away the overburden. The overburden is made up of all the soil and rocks that form a layer above the fossil. This is the hardest part of the dig. The overburden here is 12 feet deep!

Everyone is working with picks and shovels and wheelbarrows. It's boring, exhausting work. The heat here is incredible. It's about 100°. When the breeze stops, you feel like you're a pizza sitting on a rock.

> How would you describe Day 1 and Day 2 of the dig?

The bones of the neck are still together after millions of years.

Partner Jigsaw Technique Read a section of Nate Murphy and the Mystery Sauropod with a partner. Write down one category for classifying the information you read. Be prepared to summarize your section and share how you categorized the information.

Day 3

Today we start excavating the neck bones. We had discovered part of the neck on last year's dig. Now, fragment by fragment, we take away chunks of earth to reveal each bone. As we remove more and more earth, we realize we've hit pay dirt!

The bones of the neck are still all in place! The bones seem to be just as they were when the dinosaur fell into the earth millions of years ago. This is VERY unusual.

Probably 99% of all dinosaur fossils are not found like this. Usually the bones are scattered all over an area. Once they're out of the ground, scientists fit them together like a puzzle.

Everyone's excited. With every piece of earth we move away, we're looking for the next bone. At the end of the day about 12 feet of neck is showing.

Why is this dig different from other dinosaur finds?

Day 4

Everyone is up early. We're digging out the smaller bones at the top of the neck. As we uncover each new bone, we hold our breath. Will we find the skull, the rarest of dinosaur trophies?

The neck is uncovered. Will the skull be attached? We dig down, down, down. Nothing. There's nothing there. I could feel the wind get knocked out of the team. We all know that the skull usually isn't found with a skeleton. But this has been such an unusual dig, so we were all hoping to find it. The team continues to clear the earth from the neck.

"Is this anything?" a team member asks, looking down.

Another gasps, "You found the skull!"

How do you think Nate Murphy and his team would classify their activities on this day?

Everyone rushes over. Pointing towards the sky is a row of teeth that look like big, black spatulas. Here is the skull, just 18 inches from the neck! And it is complete—round and intact. Usually skulls are found smashed flat, like pancakes.

I've never seen a more excited group than the team at the campfire tonight. It doesn't seem we'll ever stop talking about today's discovery. We sing, play games, and look at the stars. What a day!

Compare and contrast this firsthand account with the selection, "T. Rex Sue Sold to Field Museum." Describe the difference in focus and information provided.

Nate cleans off the skull.

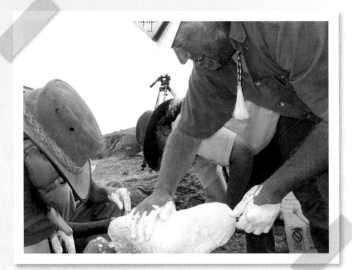
The team jackets the bones.

Day 5

Today we jacket the bones so they can be moved. Jacketing is a method of encasing the bones in plaster-soaked burlap so they don't move or break. Someone mixes the plaster. Another cuts the burlap into big strips. A third person dips the strips in the plaster. The last person applies it to the top of the fossil. It's a lot like putting a cast on a broken leg. Soon the fossils are ready to go to the museum.

We pack up our camp and head to town. What started as a group of strangers just five days ago now feels like old friends. I can't believe how fortunate I've been!

Back at the Museum: Fall 2005

The dig is over, but most of the work is just starting. It takes a long time before a fossil is ready to be shown in a museum. I'm working with other scientists in the museum's dinosaur lab. We've opening up the skull jacket. I can't wait. It's time to start unraveling the mystery!

We carefully remove the plaster and look at the skull right-side-up for the first time. Then we realize we are gazing upon a dinosaur that's made paleontological history.

Why would categories be important to scientists in putting a skeleton together for display in a museum?

Mystery Sauropod Dig: Summer 2005

Day 1: The team arrives at the ranch in Montana.

Day 2: The team clears the overburden with picks and shovels.

Day 3: The neck bones are uncovered.

Day 4: The skull is revealed!

Day 5: The team jackets the bones so they can travel.

Think and Respond

Reflect and Write

- You and your partner have read a section of *Nate Murphy and the Mystery Sauropod*. Discuss with your partner the information you read and the categories you could use to classify the information.

- Work with your partner to write down the names of your categories on one side of an index card. Then on the other side write important information about each category. Finally share your answers with other partner pairs who have read different sections.

Compound Words in Context

Search through *Nate Murphy and the Mystery Sauropod* for compound words, and list them. With a partner, discuss the meanings of the smaller words and how they relate to the meaning of each compound word. Then write sentences about what it would be like to go on a dinosaur dig. Use as many compound words as you can.

Turn and Talk

SYNTHESIZE: CLASSIFY/CATEGORIZE INFORMATION

Discuss with a partner what you have learned so far about how to classify and categorize the important information in a selection.

- How do you decide what categories to use to group the most important ideas and information in a passage?

Discuss with a partner how you could classify the information in *Nate Murphy and the Mystery Sauropod*.

Critical Thinking

In a group, brainstorm a list of what fossil hunters do. Write your ideas on one side of a sheet of paper. Look back through *Nate Murphy and the Mystery Sauropod*. Write down the steps that the fossil hunters followed. Then answer these questions.

- Why do fossil hunters follow certain steps in their work?

- How do you think fossil hunters feel when they finish a dig? Explain your answers.

Sauropod

In a newspaper article, an author gives the reader information about a recent event by answering the 5 W questions: *who, what, when, where,* and *why.* In this newspaper article, Madelyn writes about a newly discovered dinosaur.

Missing Link on Display
by Madelyn Najar

Ghost Ranch, NM—This weekend, the Southwest Natural History Museum will unveil fossils from an unusual discovery. Visitors will have the chance to see a "buck-toothed, evil spirit." That's how museum director Dr. David Markson describes this dinosaur, which was previously unheard of. He's not alone in his description.

The writer clearly introduces the topic and focus of the newspaper article.

"The Latin name it was given is quite long," says Dr. Markson. "It translates to 'Evil Spirit Buck-Toothed Reptile.' That's a pretty accurate name, if you ask me."

This newly-identified dinosaur was discovered in Ghost Ranch, New Mexico. Its hometown inspired its creepy name. Even though parts of its skull and neck are missing, scientists can tell a lot about it. For example, it probably measured about four feet long. Its snout was short. It had long, sharp teeth.

The writer groups related information together.

Scientists were surprised when they learned the dinosaur was a carnivore, or meat eater. That's because it lived over 205 million years ago!

"It's amazing how old the remains are," says Dr. Markson. "We're still learning a lot about this dinosaur because it's such a new discovery. Everything tells us he's the missing link."

The writer provides accurate quotes from a primary source.

This "missing link" fills a great gap in time. The gap starts with the oldest-known dinosaurs. It ends with advanced dinosaurs, like *Tyrannosaurus rex.* There aren't a lot of fossil records to show what dinosaurs were like in between.

"Ah! That's what makes this evil, buck-toothed spirit so special!" says Dr. Markson. "He will tell us a lot about the time period and dinosaur history. He'll also teach us about what life was like in New Mexico a couple hundred million years ago!"

The writer concludes with a strong statement that shows why the topic is meaningful.

Respond in Writing

Answer these questions about the newspaper article you just read.

- What are the 5 Ws for this newspaper article, and how did each help you understand the topic? Use examples from the article to support your answer.

- Describe how the photos presented with this article help to clarify the event in this article. Compare and contrast the photos with the text.

Writing: Newspaper Article

Use the steps of the writing process to create your own newspaper article. The following tips can help you make your writing its best.

Prewriting

- Gather important facts and details about the 5 Ws for your newspaper article.

- Research your topic in books and on the Internet.

- Interview someone related to your article's topic and take careful notes. For an even stronger article, compare and contrast the information you received from your interview with a secondhand account of the topic. Describe the differences in focus and information you gather.

Drafting

- Write a clear and catchy lead that will capture your audience's attention.

- Group information that is alike or connected together in paragraphs. Give the most important information first. Then move to interesting, but less important, details.

- Sprinkle in quotes from your interview or research to make your article more interesting.

Revising

- Make sure your beginning, or lead, answers the 5 W questions.
- Check your organization, and move any details that are out of order.
- Refer to your prewriting to make sure you didn't leave out important details. Use sticky notes to add missing details, as necessary.
- Remember to use a variety of sentence types to make your writing more interesting.

Editing

- Check your article for correct use of subordinate conjunctions.
- Look closely at your independent and dependent clauses. Make sure your sentences are complete and correctly punctuated.
- Check that you've used relative pronouns correctly in your sentences.
- Read your article slowly. Hold a blank piece of paper under the line you are reading to focus your attention on one part at a time.

Publishing

- Top your article with a clever headline.
- Add a photograph or illustration that helps clarify information in your article.
- Consider submitting your article to your school newspaper or a community newsletter.

Contents

Wearing Away

Modeled Reading

Shared Reading

Interactive Reading

Writing

GRAND CANYON

A Trail Through Time

Linda Vieira

Illustrations by
Christopher Canyon

Appreciative Listening

Appreciative listening means you listen for particular words or phrases you enjoy hearing in the text. Listen to the focus questions your teacher will read to you.

VISIT
Arches National Park
Gateway to the Past

ARCHES NATIONAL PARK

Where Is the Park?

Arches National Park is located near Moab, Utah, not far from the Colorado River.

History in Stone

The park's arches were created over thousands of years as weather wore away layers of rock. Some of the layers of rock were soft and broke apart easily. But the **composition** of other layers of rock was harder. The hard rock stayed in place even as softer rock wore away. This **erosion** created the arches you see today.

Salt Lake City ✪
Provo •
Arches National Park ■
Moab •

A Rich History

For centuries people have been attracted to the **splendor** of this land. **Ancient** peoples arrived about 10,000 years ago. The Pueblo and Fremont tribes settled here almost 2,000 years ago. Then, in the late 1700s, Spanish explorers visited the area.

Places to See

- Be sure to visit Elephant Butte, the highest spot in the park.

- Don't miss Landscape Arch, the park's most **significant** arch. More than 300 feet long, it is one of the longest arches in North America.

Structured Vocabulary Discussion

When your teacher says a vocabulary word, you and your partner should each write down the first words you think of on a piece of paper. When your teacher says, "Stop," exchange papers with your partner and explain any of the words on your lists to each other.

Throughout the week, add to your vocabulary journal entries. Record new insights and other words that relate to this week's vocabulary.

Picture It

Draw a chart like this in your vocabulary journal. Give examples of things you think of as **ancient**.

```
              ┌─────────────┐
              │    earth     │
              └─────────────┘
┌─────────┐   ┌─────────────┐
│ ancient │───│             │
└─────────┘   └─────────────┘
              ┌─────────────┐
              │             │
              └─────────────┘
```

Draw a chart like this in your vocabulary journal. What causes **erosion**? Fill in the boxes with the answer.

What causes erosion?

moving water

Ask Questions

Meaning

Asking questions keeps you thinking about what you are reading. Even before you begin reading, ask questions to make predictions about the text. As you read, ask questions to help you connect new ideas and information. After reading, ask questions to help you summarize what you read.

ASKING QUESTIONS helps you to understand text better.

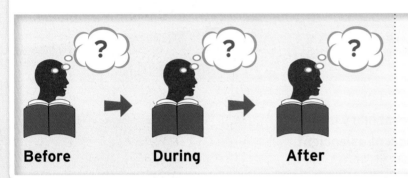

Before   During   After

Think of questions before, during, and after you read.

TURN AND TALK Listen to your teacher read the following lines below from *Grand Canyon: A Trail Through Time*. Think of questions as you read. When you finish reading, discuss your questions with your partner. Read these suggestions for questions to ask about the selection.

• You might ask to find out more about the Colorado River.

• You might ask to find out more about the "cycle of eroding rock" described in the first sentence.

The endless cycle of eroding rock and moving water carved the Grand Canyon millions of years ago. Blustering wind and pounding rain continue to widen it, grinding down rocks that used to be mountains and volcanoes. The rushing Colorado River deepens this natural wonder, dragging rocks and mud along its path through ancient plains and lava flows.

TAKE IT WITH YOU Ask questions to help you understand the text you are reading. As you read other selections, try to think of questions that will guide you before, during, and after reading. Use a chart like the one below to see questions that one student asked.

Questions About Meaning

Preview (Before Reading)

Where is the Grand Canyon?

Pause (During Reading)

In the Text

The eroding rock and moving water carved out the Grand Canyon.

Questions About Meaning

What is eroding rock?

How does a river carve out rock?

Reflect (After Reading)

Questions About Meaning

Are there other places like the Grand Canyon?

How long did the process take to form the Grand Canyon?

SAVING MAMMOTH CAVE

By Allison Welch

In 1929 many Americans lost their jobs. In 1933 President Roosevelt created the Civilian Conservation Corps (CCC) to give people work. Nicknamed "Roosevelt's Tree Army," the CCC worked to save our natural resources. One of the first projects of the CCC was Mammoth Cave National Park.

From the Diary of Nathan Culver

August 26, 1935

Today I was accepted into the CCC. I'm glad because in the CCC I will earn money to send to my parents. I know this will work out for me.

September 9, 1935

I arrived at Army headquarters to register for the CCC. I was assigned to Mammoth Cave in Kentucky. As soon as I stepped on the bus, I noticed it was full of men about my age, 19. Everyone looked as nervous as I did!

September 13, 1935

So far, life at Mammoth Cave is fun. At night we play sports, listen to the radio, or read. Today I learned that caves are formed by water washing away, or eroding, rock for thousands of years. A park guide told us Mammoth Cave is the longest cave in the world!

September 16, 1935

Today our foreman showed us the cave entrance. The runoff from a nearby field is clogging it with soil. Our job is to plant trees to stop the erosion. It will take hard work, but the trees will be beautiful and protect the cave entrance.

November 15, 1935

My camp has been cutting brush to prevent fires and planting trees to prevent erosion. But the best job has been creating trails inside the cave. The cave has amazing rock formations. The rock's composition is mostly limestone. Many unusual animals live in the cave, such as eyeless fish.

December 9, 1935

What an exciting day! While we were working on the trails, our park guides found the remains of someone who lived long ago. We helped move a boulder off the trapped remains so scientists can study the find.

September 26, 1936

We will be in a parade in Cave City today. On Monday, my job at the cave will end. I am eager to see my family, but I am proud of my work to protect this significant American landmark.

Experiment: Erosion in ACTION

What happens to the plants and soil when strong winds blow or heavy rains fall? Here is an experiment to find out.

You will need

- a paper plate
- dry soil, small rocks, leaves, and twigs
- spray bottle with water

Steps:

1. Pile soil on the plate. Pat rocks, leaves, and twigs into the soil. Did you know as you are patting the rocks, leaves, and twigs into the soil, you are making a landform? Did you know that cutting down trees and plants can cause erosion?

2. Blow gently on the landform. Slowly begin to blow harder to show how strong winds shape the land. What happens to the soil when the rocks, leaves, and twigs are whipped around by the wind? Erosion takes place when wind and water carry away the soil, rocks, and plants on the land.

3. Use the bottle to spray "rain" onto your landform for about one minute. What happens? The buildup of soil and rocks can cause streams to become clogged.

Consonant Doubling

Activity One

About Consonant Doubling

Some words, such as *pop* and *hot*, have a consonant-vowel-consonant (CVC) pattern. To add a suffix to many CVC words, double the second consonant before adding the suffix. For example, *pop* + *p* + *ing* = *popping* and
hot + *t* + *est* = *hottest*.

Consonant Doubling in Context

With a small group, read back through the experiment to find words in which the final consonant was doubled. Make a chart like the one below to show what you found.

CVC WORD PATTERN	ENDING	FINAL WORD
pat	-ing	patting

Activity Two

Explore Words Together

Work with a partner to add endings such as -*er*, -*ed*, -*est*, or -*ing* to each word on the right. Then think of other words with which you could use the double consonant rule. Share your lists with the class.

grab	drop
fat	tug
zip	pet

Activity Three

Explore Words in Writing

Look back at the experiment on page 544. Write a paragraph that explains the steps in erosion. Share your explanation with a partner. Use words with the CVC pattern. Have your partner find and circle the words with doubled final consonants.

RACE AGAINST TIME:
David Sucec Records
ANCIENT ART

An Interview with David Sucec by Michelle Budzilowicz

Imagine you are on a class trip to an art museum. When you step off the bus, you are in Utah's Horseshoe Canyon. But no buildings are here. Where is the art?

The art is painted right on the canyon walls! Thousands of years ago, Utah's earliest artists filled these canyons with unique paintings. Art historian David Sucec wants to record this ancient art. He hopes to collect images of all the paintings before erosion and weathering erase them forever.

David is in a race against time. As time passes, nature wears away the paintings. People have damaged some paintings, too.

There are more than 400 sites. Some sites have many paintings. It won't be easy. Learn what David Sucec has to say about this amazing project.

What questions do you have before you begin reading about David Sucec's work with this ancient art?

Why did you start recording ancient rock art?

Photographer Craig Law and I realized that we needed to map and record Utah's ancient rock art. We knew that if we did not record it soon, erosion and human damage would take it all away. In 1991, we began to record the art. So far we have photographed 289 sites of ancient images.

Who made this ancient art? Where do you find it?

We do not know the artists' names. But we do know that they were hunters and gatherers. They began their work between 7,000 and 9,000 years ago. They disappeared between 1,300 and 1,500 years ago. These artists lived in Utah, Colorado, and Arizona.

What question could you ask to understand more about this style of art?

How did the artists create the images?

The artists painted with brushes, fingertips, hands, and cloth. They also chipped lines and zigzags into the art. Some art is just pecked into the wall with no paint. Some has been drawn onto the rock walls with charcoal.

The artists painted using a variety of reds and whites. Sometimes they used green, yellow, blue, or black.

Reverse Think-Aloud Technique
Listen as your partner reads part of the text aloud. Choose a point in the text to stop your partner and ask what he or she is thinking about the text at that moment. Then switch roles with your partner.

What does the art show about the people who made it?

This kind of art is one of two major painted rock art styles in the United States from that early time period. The paintings are detailed. By studying these ancient pictures and drawings, we know that it is the work of advanced humans. They are not just plain figures drawn by simple people as some previous European Americans thought.

We are trying to unlock the mysteries of these paintings.

What are the natural dangers to the art?

Almost all the art is found on sandstone walls. Winds break down and weather the sandstone. Water often freezes and thaws in the cracks of the walls. Then the rock erodes. Some colors, particularly white, fade with time.

How is the erosion to this ancient art like other erosion you have read about?

How do people threaten the art?

Graffiti and theft have hurt the art. Luckily, these things are no longer as common as they were in the past. These crimes leave scars on the art. They cause more damage than natural weathering.

How do you record the art?

Craig Law uses a special large-format camera. It gives us the clearest, most detailed pictures of the art. We also need to draw some of the art to record every detail.

Do you have any favorite art?

If I had to choose one, it would be the work called the Holy Ghost Group. The locals here in Utah named it years ago. The drawings look like large spirit figures.

What makes this group special is its size and height. The figures look real. We used to think that the Greeks were the first to paint like this around 2,300 years ago. But the Holy Ghost Group was probably painted much before that, around 4,000 years ago!

If you could interview David Sucec, what question would you ask?

What will you do with the art you record?

The final collection of photographs, drawings, and information will go to the University of Utah. Large museums may have exhibits of the work, too.

What got you interested in this job?

I've been interested in Native Americans since I was in the Boy Scouts. I got involved in photography when I was in college.

What is your favorite part of the job?

I like being in the canyons. They are often wild places untouched by humans. I love suddenly finding a rock art site, especially when I did not know it was there.

How can people help protect this ancient art?

To protect the art, we cannot touch it. The oils in our skin affect the art. In less than 15 minutes, one person can do more damage to a rock art panel than thousands of years of erosion. We need to respect this art from an ancient people.

What questions could you ask to find out about other kinds of ancient art?

Think and Respond

Reflect and Write

- You and your partner took turns reading *Race Against Time* aloud. You asked questions about the text as you read. Discuss these questions with your partner.

- On one side of an index card, write down one question that you asked. On the other side, write down the answer that you and your partner discussed.

Consonant Doubling in Context

Search through *Race Against Time* to find CVC words. List the words and circle any to which you could add an -er, -est, -ed, or -ing ending. Use what you know about consonant doubling to rewrite those words with new endings.

Turn and Talk

ASK QUESTIONS: MEANING

Discuss with your partner why asking questions about what you read is an important strategy.

- Why is it important to ask those questions you have in your mind as you read?

Choose one question you asked as you read this week's selections. Share your question with a partner.

Critical Thinking

Think about David Sucec's effort to record ancient canyon art. With your partner, discuss why David Sucec believes it is important to save this ancient rock art. Write two reasons why the art is in danger of being lost.

Then discuss these questions.

- Why is David Sucec's effort to save ancient canyon art like a race?

- What other projects do you know of in which people are racing to save something that is in danger?

- How are their efforts similar to Sucec's? How are they different?

Vocabulary

Our OLD FRIEND Is Really Gone!

http://www.friendsoftheoldman

Posted: May 11, 2003

Last week the Old Man of the Mountain crumbled and fell from Franconia Notch. The Old Man was an important symbol for New Hampshire.

My family and I visited the Old Man last summer. We could see his big face sticking out of the rock. My dad said that a **glacier** covered these mountains long ago. When the huge sheets of ice moved, they carved the Old Man's face from the stone.

People have known for a long time that the face was **weathering**. They even tried to fix it with cement, but they couldn't **prevent** the Old Man from crumbling.

I took a **survey** at school to find out if people thought the face should be rebuilt to its **previous** shape. My classmates said no. We are all sad that the Old Man is gone. Even mountains must change sooner or later!

—Julie Velarde, age 9

Structured Vocabulary Discussion

As your teacher says a vocabulary word, you and your partner write down the first words you think of on a piece of paper. When you teacher says "Stop," exchange papers with your partner and share the words on your lists with each other.

Throughout the week, add to your vocabulary journal entries. Record new insights and other words that relate to this week's vocabulary.

Picture It

Draw a word web like this in your vocabulary journal. Give examples of things you can **prevent**.

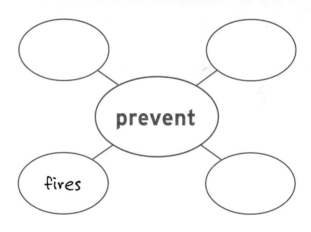

Draw a circle like this in your vocabulary journal. Fill in the circle with words for places where **weathering** might occur.

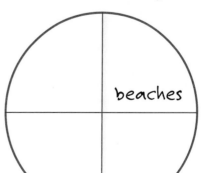

Swept Away

by Colin Tracy

You know that erosion can shape land over thousands of years. Did you know erosion can also change the shape of the land very quickly? Fast-moving storms can sweep away roads, beaches, and neighborhoods. These photos, from a survey by the U.S. government, show us how.

September 1998

For years, the coastal beauty of Bay St. Louis, Mississippi, attracted many visitors.

August 2005

Hurricane Katrina changed Bay St. Louis forever. Powerful winds destroyed houses and even ripped the leaves off the trees!

July 2001

In 2001 Dauphin Island, Mississippi, was home to quiet neighborhoods like this one.

September 2004

Dauphin Island changed when Hurricanes Lili and Ivan passed through. Plants and land swept out to sea. Roads and driveways disappeared.

August 2005

Hurricane Katrina did even more damage to the island. Giant waves washed the land from under people's homes and left rotting planks behind. Much of the beach is gone.

Letter from the Dust Bowl

May 1, 1935

Dear Rose,

   I'm sorry it has been so long since I last wrote. Our trip to California took a long time.

   We were sad to leave our farm, but the dust storms drove us away. When we first moved to Oklahoma, we grew golden wheat. Then the rains stopped. The wheat died. There was nothing to hold down the soil, so it blew away in the wind. That's why Oklahoma is one of the states in the "Dust Bowl."

   The dust storms were like blizzards, only with dirt instead of snow. The dust stung our faces and got in everything. One time, the dust was so thick I couldn't see my hand in front of me. After the worst storm, we left for California.

   Now we live in a beautiful farming town. I like California, but I hope that one day Oklahoma will be a land of golden wheat again.

   Love,

   Betty

Irregular Verbs

Activity One

About Irregular Verbs

A regular verb ends in *-d* or *-ed* to show action in the past. Irregular verbs change form in the past tense. They do not end in *-d* or *-ed*. For example: *speak/spoke, know/knew, run/ran*.

Irregular Verbs in Context

With a partner read Betty's letter again. Make a chart like the one below to show the irregular verbs you find.

PRESENT TENSE	PAST TENSE
write	wrote

Activity Two

Explore Words Together

Look at the words on the right with a partner. Work together to write pairs of sentences. Write one sentence using the verb in the present tense and one using the verb in the past tense.

go	feed
run	come
drink	swim

Activity Three

Explore Words in Writing

Write a letter about a time that you had to leave or move from one place to another. Include several irregular verbs. Then exchange letters with a partner. Read your partner's letter and find the irregular verbs.

The Case of the Missing Capsule

by Katie Smith

We were all taking out our science books one Friday afternoon when Mrs. Napoli announced she had a surprise.

"Psst, Emma. That means pop quiz," my best friend Latanya whispered. "Did you do your reading?"

Our last reading had been about erosion and glaciers, so I tried to remember what I read the night before . . . *Glacier . . . a slow moving block of ice.*

"No need to panic," Mrs. Napoli said. "The surprise is in this envelope, which is addressed to our class."

We all breathed a sigh of relief as Mrs. Napoli held up an envelope. On it written in bold, black letters were the words . . . ***Fourth Graders of 2008***.

Mrs. Napoli said, "This letter has been kept for us in the library for the past 50 years.

May 1, 1958

Dear Fourth Graders of 2008,

Hello from fifty years ago! We have buried a time capsule with items from 1958.

You will also find items from 1908. Back then, the fourth grade class made a time capsule to celebrate the opening of this school. Now it is your turn. You can add your items and rebury the capsule for the class of 2058.

Enclosed is a map that shows where we buried our time capsule. Happy hunting!

Your friends from the past,

Fourth Graders of 1958

What kind of information does the letter give you?

558

Mrs. Napoli passed out compasses, shovels, copies of the map, and a tape measure. Then we followed the directions on the map, but we were surprised by what we saw. The "spot" was in the middle of a ditch.

"This looks like a ramp," said Jordan. "I wish I had my board."

I rolled my eyes. Jordan always brought up skateboarding. Mrs. Napoli looked at the map, checked her compass, and measured again. "It looks like you read the map correctly," she stated, "although this doesn't seem like the right place."

Why is the map an important part of the story?

We decided to dig anyway, but after digging for an hour all we found was dirt. The capsule was officially missing!

The capsule could be anywhere, so we decided to put our heads together and find out what happened to it.

Find the Great Oak Tree behind the school.

Stand on the east side of the tree.

Measure 20 feet due east of the tree.

✗ marks the spot.

Dig 1 foot down to uncover the past!

Read, Cover, Remember, Retell Technique With a partner, take turns reading as much text as you can cover with your hand. Then cover up what you read and retell the information to your partner.

"Let's record our clues," I said. There wasn't much to record at first, but then Jake gave us a step in the right direction.

"It looks like water used to flow through here," he said. "We have something similar behind our house. It's kind of like a creek, but it only fills up after a storm."

"Why would they bury the capsule in a creek?" Latanya asked.

"Maybe it wasn't a creek in 1958," Jake said. "The one in our yard got larger after that hurricane a few years ago. You know, it's erosion. Water may have washed away the soil and carved a path in the earth."

"Ah-ha, erosion," I said, and wrote the word in my notebook. "I think you're onto something, Jake."

What makes this story a mystery?

"Why don't you go to the library? You could research to find out what has happened on school grounds over the past fifty years," Mrs. Napoli said.

It sounded like a good plan, so a group of us headed to the library after school.

At the library we split up. Jake and I went to research maps. Latanya, Jordan, and Madison focused on reading old newspapers for leads on major storms.

After a while, the clues came together. First Jake and I realized that the boundary of our school property was once the path of a stream called School Creek. Then we suddenly heard an exclamation from Latanya.

"I think I've uncovered exactly what we've been looking for!" she said. "There was a hurricane in 1960 that slammed our area. Look at this article."

Because of the swelling floodwaters from Hurricane Donna, crews built a makeshift dam out of stone and rock behind South Shore Elementary School. Luckily, the dam helped prevent the water from flooding the town square.

"School Creek must have flooded, and the water probably washed away the soil and the time capsule," Jake said. "Now we'll never know where the capsule went!"

"Look at the picture," Latanya said. It showed our very own creek filled up with water, and at the end of it was a small stone dam.

"That's the old wall by the baseball field!" I said. "Do you think the capsule is near the wall?"

"There's only one way to find out," said Jake.

What is the important clue from the newspaper article?

561

On Monday, we went to the maintenance room and told Mr. Chen about our search. He came with us to the old dam. First, he poked around and then, suddenly, we heard the clink of metal.

"Hold on," said Mr. Chen. "There's something here."

We cheered. We had found the capsule, but the items were still a mystery. Inside we found an ad for a new color TV. There was also a picture of Elvis Presley. From 1908 we found a car ad for the brand-new Model T and some tea bags that were falling apart. A note said that tea bags were a new invention in 1908.

As we looked at the items from 1908, Madison said, "When we rebury this we should put it in a place that's safe from erosion."

"How about burying it between the roots of the Great Oak Tree," suggested Jordan. "It will be easy to find, and the roots will help keep the soil from eroding."

"What if something happens to the tree?" Latanya asked.

"The changing landscape didn't stop us," I said with a smile.

"The class of 2058 may have their own mystery to solve!"

What do the students learn from the mystery items?

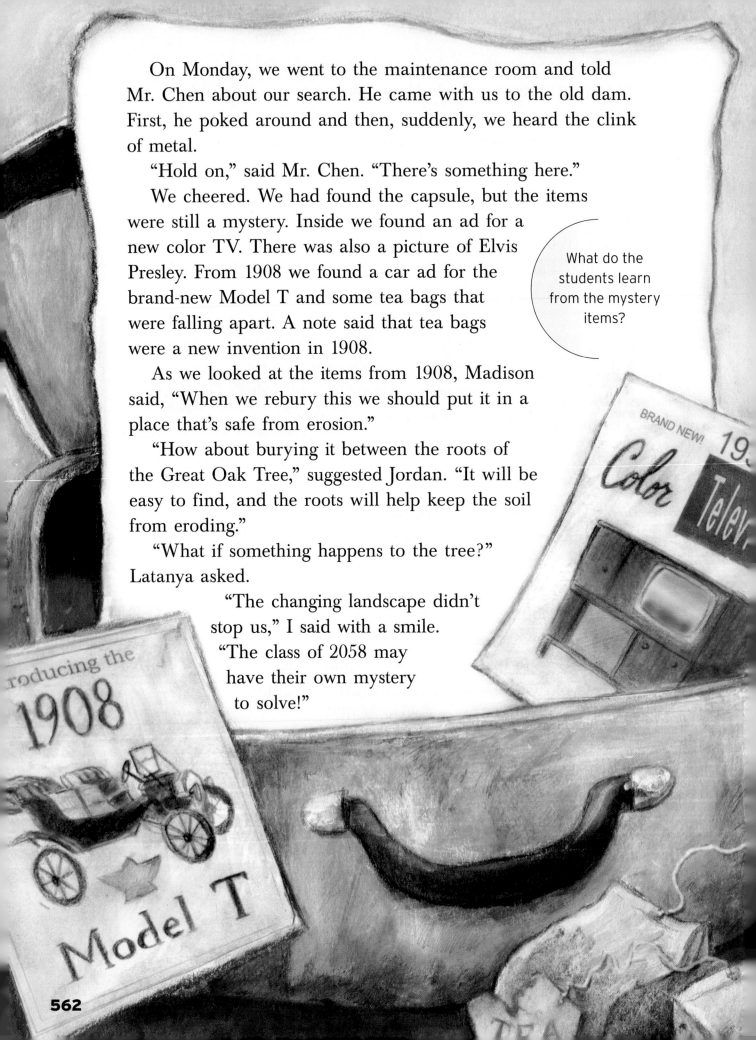

562

Think and Respond

Reflect and Write

- You and your partner took turns retelling parts of *The Case of the Missing Capsule* as you read. Discuss why the story is a mystery.

- On one side of an index card, write words that describe a mystery. On the other side of the card, write a part from the story *The Case of the Missing Capsule* that fits that description.

Irregular Verbs in Context

Search through *The Case of the Missing Capsule* for irregular verbs. List the verbs and share them with a partner. Then write sentences about erosion and weathering. Use one irregular verb in each sentence.

Turn and Talk

MONITOR UNDERSTANDING: GENRE

In small groups discuss why knowing about the genre is an important strategy to help in understanding text.

- How does knowing about the genre help you understand a selection?

- To help you use genre to support meaning and understanding, think about these questions with a partner: *What makes a story a mystery? What are the story elements in a mystery?*

Critical Thinking

Think about the mystery in *The Case of the Missing Capsule*. With a partner, discuss how the students used their knowledge to figure out where the time capsule could be found. Write a few sentences describing how erosion played a role in solving the mystery. Then, discuss these questions:

- What caused the erosion in the schoolyard?

- Why wasn't the time capsule where the map said it would be?

Your favorite music of 1958

In a story, an author writes about characters and events that are fictional, or make-believe. In this story, Antonio combines fiction and fact by writing a story about a real cave in Calaveras County, California.

Down in Moaning Cavern
by Antonio de la Fuente

"Dad, can we go today?" Jesse pleaded, as he shook his dad's arms. "Please? Moaning Cavern is sooooo close!"

> The writer uses dialogue to show the responses of each character to the situation.

"OK, I hear you," his dad laughed, patting Jesse's buzz cut. "Let's roll."

"Yes!" yelled Jesse. "You're totally awesome, Dad." Jesse had read how, in 1922, some men wanted to give tours of Moaning Cavern. So, they built a huge spiral staircase down into the cave. Jesse wanted to hear the cave moan, too. The moaning sound came through the holes in the stone!

When they got there, Jesse looked down the 100-foot spiral staircase. He suddenly felt dizzy. "Dad, wait. I don't feel well," he said, stopping near the cave's entrance.

> The writer clearly introduces a challenge the main character must face.

Just then, a woman hugged her elderly father in a wheelchair nearby. "Happy 100th birthday, Dad. We're here!" Jesse and his dad turned to wish the man a happy birthday.

The man spoke slowly. "I was 10 years old when my father lowered me into this cavern in an ore bucket," he told Jesse, recalling the memory. "I lit a candle. What I saw had no end. That was 1922."

"Wow." Jesse's brown eyes widened. "What were you doing?"

"My father led the team that built this staircase," said the man. "I helped occasionally. Some of his men worked at the bottom of the cave. Others worked up top. They bridged a gap as tall as the Statue of Liberty. By the way," the man whispered to Jesse, "I know these steps were made from an old World War I battleship. They're solid steel. Very safe," he said with a wink.

Jesse was amazed by the man's boyhood memories. The man had helped Jesse forget his fear. "I feel better, Dad. No stopping now!"

The writer uses precise details to develop events and describe the setting.

The writer includes a strong ending that shows how the main character's problem is resolved.

Respond in Writing

Answer these questions about the story you just read.

- How do dialogue and description help develop the events of this story? In what way do they help show how the narrator feels about the experience he's describing? Support your answer with examples from the story.

- Which descriptions help you picture the characters? Pick three strong word choices, and describe how they help you.

Writing: Story

Use the steps of the writing process to create your own story.
The following tips can help you make your writing its best.

Prewriting

- Select a specific person or event as a topic. Then think about your setting. Remember that your character, topic, and setting can be based on real people, events, and places, but that you should add details to make them your own.

- Brainstorm a list of interesting problems and choose one that your main character will face.

- Make quick sketches to plan the sequence of your plot.

Drafting

- During the drafting of your story, close your eyes occasionally to help you better imagine the events you plan to capture in words. Write descriptively about the characters, actions, and setting you picture in your mind.

- Use dialogue to show your characters' personalities and to show how they respond to situations in your story.

My story topic:

My main character:

The setting:

The main problem:

The plot:

Revising

- Ask yourself if each event in your story naturally builds tension and leads to the next event.

- Remember to use a variety of sentence types and beginnings to make your writing more interesting.

- Read your work to a partner. Ask if any parts of your story are unclear or need more explanation.

Editing

- Read closely to check for homophone spelling errors or commonly misused words.

- Make sure your verbs agree with their subjects and that you have used irregular verbs correctly.

- Use your resources. Keep a dictionary and Writer's Handbook ready while you are editing. You don't have to memorize every rule, as long as you know how to locate information when you need it.

Publishing

- Consider adding an illustration of the most important scene in your story.

- Create a clean final copy of your story to share with friends and family.

Glossary

Using the Glossary

Like a dictionary, this glossary lists words in alphabetical order. Guide words at the top of each page show you the first and last word on the page. If a word has more than one syllable, the syllables are separated by a dark dot (•). Use the pronunciation key on the bottom of every other page.

Sample

The pronunciation guide shows how to say the word. The accent shows which syllable is stressed.

The part of speech shows how the word is often used.

Each word is broken into syllables.

con•ser•va•tory (kən sur′ və tôr′ ē) *n.* A glass room for growing and showing plants. *The **conservatory** was filled with plants from around the world.*

The definition shows what the word means.

The example sentence includes the word in it.

Abbreviations: *adj.* adjective, *adv.* adverb, *conj.* conjunction, *interj.* interjection, *n.* noun, *prep.* preposition, *pron.* pronoun, *v.* verb

af•fec•tion•ate (ə fek′ shən it) *adj.* Loving. *Joe's dog is very **affectionate**.*

a•muse•ment (ə myo͞oz′ mənt) *n.* Entertainment. *The park had rides and other forms of **amusement**.*

as•sem•bled (ə sem′ bəld) *v.* To bring people or things together. *The math club **assembled** for practice.*

at•tached (ə tach′ d) *v.* Fastened by sticking or tying. *Sophie **attached** a string to her kite.*

bi•ol•ogy (bī äl′ ə jē) *n.* The study of living organisms, such as plants and animals. *My sister signed up to study **biology** at her high school.*

bliz•zard (bliz′ ərd) *n.* A long snowstorm with strong winds. *The **blizzard** covered our house with snow.*

cap•sule (kap′ səl) *n.* Sealed box or package. *The students prepared a time **capsule** for their class project in history.*

car•bon di•ox•ide (kär′ bən dī äks′ īd) *n.* Colorless gas we breathe out. *Plants need **carbon dioxide** to live.*

ce•ment (sə ment′) *n.* Mixture of powders that hardens when it dries. *Workers poured **cement** to make a sidewalk along the street.*

char•i•ty (char′ i tē) *n.* Helpfulness towards others, especially those in need. *The Clarks believed in **charity**, so they gave away their old clothes.*

clings (klingz) *v.* Holds on tightly. *Liz clings to the railing when she crosses over a high bridge.*

com·plain (kəm plān´) *v.* **complained** To say you are unhappy. *Susie complained because she was so cold.*

con·stant·ly (kän´ stənt lē) *adv.* Always staying the same. *Ben was constantly studying his math.*

con·struct (kən strukt´) *v.* To make by putting parts together. *Grandpa showed us how to construct a kite.*

crea·tiv·i·ty (krē´ ā tɪv´ ə tē) *n.* To use your imagination for new ideas. *Mrs. Decker's fourth grade class showed their creativity in their class projects.*

cu·ra·tor (kyoo rā´ tər) *n.* Person who cares for a museum, zoo, or other place. *The curator of the museum chose the paintings.*

de·pres·sion (dē presh´ ən) *n.* Low place or area. *Water collected in a depression in the ground.*

des·per·ate (des´ pər it) *adj.* Feeling a loss of hope. *The team was desperate to score a goal to avoid losing the game.*

dis·ap·point (dis´ ə point´) *v.* **disappointed** To fail to meet hopes. *The circus disappointed Lee because there were no clowns or funny cars.*

dis·con·tin·ue (dis´ kən tin´ yoo) *v.* To stop; to come to an end. *The store will discontinue the old toy.*

dis·guise (dis gīz´) *n.* Clothing or mask that makes someone look different. *The spy wore a disguise.*

dis·or·i·ent·ed (dis ôr ē en´ tid) *adj.* Confused about something, or the time or place. *Mr. Rodriguez became disoriented after he took a wrong turn.*

dis·solve (di zälv´) *v.* To melt. *To make punch, we dissolve the fruit powder in water and stir.*

ex·ca·vat·ing (ek´ skə vā´ ting) *v.* To dig out and remove. *The scientists were excavating a fossil.*

ex·haust (eg zôst´) *v.* **exhausting** Tiring. *Field Day was exhausting, but fun!*

ex·hi·bits (eg zɪb´ ɪtz) *n.* Displays for people to see. *The museum had many exhibits of paintings.*

ex·o·tic (ig zät´ ik) *adj.* From another country; foreign; otherworldly. *In Australia, we saw many exotic plants.*

fas·ci·nate (fas´ ə nāt´) *v.* To hold your attention by being interesting or delightful. *The flashy costumes were meant to fascinate us.*

fe·ro·cious (fə rō´ shəs) *adj.* Very fierce or savage. *The ferocious dog lunged at the fence.*

PRONUNCIATION KEY

a	add, map	oi	oil, boy	zh	vision, pleasure
ā	ace, rate	ou	pout, now	ə	the schwa, an
â(r)	care, air	ŏŏ	took, full		unstressed vowel
ä	palm, father	ōō	pool, food		representing the
e	end, pet	u	up, done		sound spelled
ē	equal, tree	ŧ	care, her,		*a* in *above*
i	it, give		sir, burn,		*e* in *sicken*
ī	ice, write		word		*i* in *possible*
o	odd, hot	yōō	fuse, few		*o* in *melon*
ō	open, so	z	zest, wise		*u* in *circus*
ô	order, jaw				

fer·til·ize (fʉrt′'l iz′) *v.* To add something to soil so plants will grow better. *Farmer Bill will* **fertilize** *his fields to increase the yield from his crops.*

flinch (flinch′) *v.* **flinching** To move quickly or shrink away. *The ringmaster couldn't help* **flinching** *as the lion roared.*

fo·cus (fō′ kəs) *v.* **focused** To fix on one thing; to concentrate. *Cara* **focused** *her attention on the teacher.*

fo·li·age (fō′ lē ij) *n.* Leaves, flowers, and branches. *The photographer took pictures of the green* **foliage**.

frag·ile (fraj′ əl) *adj.* Easily broken or damaged. *Jin dropped the* **fragile** *vase.*

frag·ment (frag′ mənt) *n.* Part broken off from the whole. *Andy found a* **fragment** *of a fern fossil in his backyard.*

glob·al warm·ing (glō′ bəl wôr′ ming) *n.* Rise in the earth's temperature. *Scientists believe pollution causes* **global warming**.

gor·geous (gôr′ jəs) *adj.* Glorious, magnificent. *I took a* **gorgeous** *picture of the setting sun.*

har·mo·ny (här′ mə nē) *n.* Agreement in feelings and actions; peaceful. *The tribes of the Iroquois nation lived together in peaceful* **harmony**.

harsh (härsh) *adj.* Severe or rough. *The pioneers faced a* **harsh** *journey on the Oregon Trail.*

hes·i·ta·tion (hez′ i tā′ shən) *n.* To stop or pause when you are not sure. *After some* **hesitation**, *Haibo ran for class president.*

hys·ter·i·cal·ly (hi ster′ i kəl lē) *adv.* With uncontrollable feeling or excitement. *Kiera made us laugh* **hysterically** *with her jokes.*

im·pres·sive (im pres′ iv) *adj.* Strong effect on the mind or emotions to create feelings of wonder or admiration. *The view from the top of the Grand Canyon was very* **impressive**.

in·gre·di·ents (in grē′ dē ənts) *n.* Items that make up a combination or mixture. *Flour was one of the* **ingredients** *we used to make cookies.*

in·spire (in spīr′) *v.* **inspires** To encourage. *Our coach* **inspires** *us to work hard.*

in·stant·ly (in′ stənt lē) *adv.* In an instant; immediately. *Juliana* **instantly** *smiled when she crossed the finish line.*

ka·pok (kā′ päk′) *n.* Giant tropical tree. *The* **kapok** *is the national tree of Puerto Rico.*

land·fill (land fil′) *n.* Area where trash is buried. *After the garbage man picks up our trash, he takes it to a* **landfill**.

le·mur (lē′ mər) *n.* Monkey–like animal with large eyes and a long tail that lives mostly in trees. *The* **lemur** *can be found only on Madagascar and nearby islands.*

main·tain (mān tān′) *v.* **maintaining** To keep something in good condition. *The Smiths spend a lot of time* **maintaining** *their lawn to keep it green.*

main·te·nance (mān′ tə nəns) *n.* The act of keeping something in good condition. *The trainer was responsbible for the **maintenance** of the gym equipment.*

min·i·a·ture (min′ ē ə chər) *adj.* Smaller in size or scale. *Annabelle had a **miniature** bed in her doll house.*

moist (moist) *adj.* Slightly wet; damp. *The morning dew left the grass too **moist** for a summer picnic.*

mus·sels (mus′ əls) *n.* Sea animals with a shell. *We found small **mussels** when we waded out in the tide pool.*

nec·tar (nek′ tər) *n.* sweet liquid found in flowers. *Bees collect **nectar** to make honey in their hive.*

pa·le·on·tol·o·gist (pā′ lē on tol′ ə jist) *n.* Scientist who studies fossils. *Ross wants to be a **paleontologist**.*

per·son·al·ity (pʉr′ sə nal′ ə tē) *n.* Qualities that make one person different from another. *Mrs. Nogami had a very friendly **personality**.*

pounce (pouns) *v.* **pounces** To spring or leap. *Our cat **pounces** on fireflies.*

prog·ress (präg′ res) *n.* Movement forward. *I was making good **progress** on my volcano project.*

rec·ol·lec·tions (rek′ ə lek′ shənz) *n.* Memories. *Aunt Lola told us **recollections** of her days as a singer.*

re·mote (ri mōt′) *adj.* Far away. *Mr. Radley lives in a **remote** area of the piney woods.*

smear (smir) *v.* **smeared** To rub on something sticky. *My mother **smeared** sunscreen on my arms and back.*

snout (snout) *n.* Nose and jaws of an animal. *The pig rubbed its **snout** in the mud.*

un·con·trol·la·bly (un′ kən trō′ lə blē) *adv.* Unable to be controlled or stopped. *The earthquake made the room shake **uncontrollably**.*

ves·sel (ves′ əl) *n.* Large watercraft. *The men loaded boxes and crates onto the sailing **vessel**.*

zo·ol·o·gy (zō äl′ ə jē) *n.* Study of animal life. *A ranger from the wildlife center gave a presentation on **zoology**.*

PRONUNCIATION KEY		
a add, map	oi oil, boy	zh vision, pleasure
ā ace, rate	ou pout, now	ə the schwa, an
â(r) care, air	͝o͝o took, full	unstressed vowel
ä palm, father	o͞o pool, food	representing the
e end, pet	u up, done	sound spelled
ē equal, tree	ʉ care, her,	*a* in *above*
i it, give	sir, burn,	*e* in *sicken*
ī ice, write	word	*i* in *possible*
o odd, hot	yo͞o fuse, few	*o* in *melon*
ō open, so	z zest, wise	*u* in *circus*
ô order, jaw		

Cover Acknowledgments

For permission to reprint copyrighted material, grateful acknowledgment is made to the following sources:

Dorling Kindersley/DK Publishing: Reprinted by arrangement with DK Publishing from *Boss of the Plains: The Hat That Won the West* by Laurie Carlson, illustrated by Holly Meade. Text copyright ©1998 by Holly Carlson. Illustrations copyright ©1998 by Holly Meade. All rights reserved.

Harcourt Brace & Company: Excerpt from *THE GREAT KAPOK TREE: A TALE OF THE AMAZON RAIN FOREST,* copyright ©1990 by Lynne Cherry, reprinted by permission of Harcourt, Inc.

Holiday House: Text copyright ©1991 by David A. Adler. Illustrations copyright ©1991 by John C. and Alexandra Wallner. All rights reserved. Adapted and reprinted from *A PICTURE BOOK OF CHRISTOPHER COLUMBUS* by permission of Holiday House, Inc.

Minedition, A Division of Penguin Young Readers Group: Text: From *RICKIE AND HENRI: A TRUE STORY* by Jane Goodall, illustrated by Alan Marks, copyright ©2004 by Jane Goodall, text. Copyright ©2004 by Alan Marks, illustrations. Used by permission of Minedition, A Division of Penguin Young Readers Group, A Member of Penguin Group (USA) Inc., 345 Hudson Street, New York, NY 10014. All rights reserved.

Sasquatch Books: *Eagle Boy* retold by Richard Lee Vaughan. Reprinted by permission of the publisher.

Simon & Schuster: From *DINOSAUR TREE* by Douglas Henderson. Copyright ©1994 by Douglas Henderson. Reprinted by permission of Simon & Schuster Books for Young Readers, an Imprint of Simon & Schuster Children's Publishing Division. All rights reserved. From *A BAND OF ANGELS* by Deborah Hopkinson, illustrated by Raul Colon. Text copyright ©1999 by Deborah Hopkinson copyright ©1999 by Raul Colon. Reprinted by permission of Atheneum Books for Young Readers, an Imprint of Simon and Schuster Children's Publishing Division. All rights reserved.

Walker & Company: *Grand Canyon: A Trail Through Time* by Linda Vieira, published by Walker & Company, 1997. Reprinted by permission of the publisher.

Illustration Acknowledgments

P.270a Margaret Ringia Hart/Wilkinson Studios; p.272a Margaret Ringia Hart/Wilkinson Studios; p.274a Margaret Ringia Hart/Wilkinson Studios; p.275a Margaret Ringia Hart/ Wilkinson Studios; p.276a,b,c,d Burgandy Beam/Wilkinson Studios; p.277d Burgandy Beam/ Wilkinson Studios; p.278s Linda Bittner/Wilkinson Studios; p.280a Burgandy Beam/Wilkinson Studios; p.292a Ralph Canaday/Wilkinson Studios; p.293a Ralph Canaday/Wilkinson Studios; p.296a S.G. Brooks/Wilkinson Studios; p.298b Ralph Canaday/Wilkinson Studios; p.301b Jonathan Massie/Wilkinson Studios; p.308a Julia Woolf/Wilkinson Studios; p.312a Drew Rose/ Wilkinson Studios; p.314a Drew Rose/Wilkinson Studios; p.316a Drew Rose/Wilkinson Studios; p.317a Drew Rose/Wilkinson Studios; p.324a Julie Bauknecht/Wilkinson Studios; p.330a George Hamblin/Wilkinson Studios; p.332a Burgandy Beam/Wilkinson Studios; p.334a Burgandy Beam/Wilkinson Studios; p.336a Burgandy Beam/Wilkinson Studios; p.362a George Hamblin/ Wilkinson Studios; p.374a,a Noah Clay Phipps/Wilkinson Studios; p.378a Noah Clay Phipps/ Wilkinson Studios; p.392a,b Tracy Mattocks/Wilkinson Studios; p.393c Tracy Mattocks/ Wilkinson Studios; p.394a Vicki Bradley/Wilkinson Studios; p.395a Vicki Bradley/Wilkinson Studios; p.396a Vicki Bradley/Wilkinson Studios; p.398a Vicki Bradley/Wilkinson Studios; p.399b Vicki Bradley/Wilkinson Studios; p.400a Margo Burian/Wilkinson Studios; p.402a Rob McClurkan/Wilkinson Studios; p.416b Joe Boddy/Wilkinson Studios; p.417b,b Joe Boddy/ Wilkinson Studios; p.420a Tammy Smith/Wilkinson Studios; p.427b Jonathan Massie/Wilkinson Studios; p.430c Tom Katsulis/Wilkinson Studios; p.431a Tom Katsulis/Wilkinson Studios; p.432a Jared Osterhold/Wilkinson Studios; p.436a Micha Archer/Wilkinson Studios; p.438a Micha Archer/Wilkinson Studios; p.440a Micha Archer/Wilkinson Studios; p.441b Micha Archer/ Wilkinson Studios; p.454b,d Tony Boisvert/Wilkinson Studios; p.455b Tony Boisvert/Wilkinson Studios; p.456a Dan Grant/Wilkinson Studios; p.458a Dan Grant/Wilkinson Studios; p.460a Dan Grant/Wilkinson Studios; p.461b Dan Grant/Wilkinson Studios; p.462d Franklin Ayers; p.466a,c Dennis Franzen/Wilkinson Studios; p.492a Jeff Grunewald/Wilkinson Studios; p.498a,d Jeff Hopkins/Wilkinson Studios; p.500a Jeff Hopkins/Wilkinson Studios; p.502a Jeff Hopkins/ Wilkinson Studios; p.503c Jeff Hopkins/Wilkinson Studios.

Photography Acknowledgments

P.ii ©Craig Lovell/Corbis; iii ©Stuart Westmorland/Getty Images; xi (t) ©Envision/Corbis; vii ©David Osborn/Alamy; viii (b) ©Fabio Colombini Medeiros/Animals Animals/Earth Scenes; viii (t) ©Dave King/Getty Images; ix (t) ©David Muench/Corbis; ix (b) ©Renee Lynn/Corbis; ix (c) ©Douglas Johns/Getty Images; ix (b) ©Gregory G. Dimijian, M.D./Photo Researchers, Inc.; x (cr) ©The Hoberman Collection/Alamy; x (t) ©Photographer's Choice/Rosemary Calvert/Getty Images; xii (b) ©Pascal Goetgheluck/Photo Researchers, Inc.; xii (t) ©Stockbyte/Getty Images; xii (c) ©Melba Photo Agency/Alamy; xiii (t) AP/Wide World Photos; xiii (c) ©Thomas Hallstein/ outsight.com; xiii (b) ©Darrell Gulin/Corbis; 288 The Granger Collection, New York; 290 (b) ©George H. H. Huey/Corbis; 290 (t) ©David W. Hamilton/Getty Images; 290–291 (bgd) ©Royalty-Free/Corbis; 291 (r) ©Morton Beebe/Corbis; 294 (l) ©Corel; 294 (tl) ©David W. Hamilton/Getty Images; 294 (r) Matt Straub; 295 (tr) ©PhotoDisc/Getty Images; 295 (r) ©PhotoDisc/Getty Images; 295 (l) ©PhotoDisc/Getty Images; 296 ©Purestock/SuperStock; 297 American School, (19th century). Private Collection, ©Peter Newark American Pictures/The Bridgeman Art Library; 299 (l) ©Artville/Getty Images; 301 (b) ©America 24-7/Mike Wolforth/ Getty Images; 302 ©Orjan F. Ellingvag/Corbis; 309 ©David W. Hamilton/Getty Images; 313 (tr) ©Photos.com/Jupiter Images; 314 ©Photodisc Green/The Palma Collection/Getty Images; 314–315 ©Photodisc/Getty Images; 316 (t) ©Werner Forman/Corbis; 316 (b) ©Royalty-Free/ Corbis; 317 (b) ©Comstock; 317 (t) ©Hulton Archive/Richard Harrington/Getty Images; 318 (b) ©PhotoDisc/Getty Images; 319 ©PhotoDisc/Getty Images; 320–321 (bgd) ©Houghton Mifflin Harcourt; 320 ©Gregory Bergman/Alamy Images; 321 Courtesy of the Library of Congress, LC-USF34- 082309-D; 322 (bl) ©Brand X Pictures/Jupiterimages; 322 (br) ©Artville/Getty Images; 323 (cl) ©PhotoDisc/Getty Images; 323 (br) ©Houghton Mifflin Harcourt; 324 (t) ©PhotoDisc/Getty Images; 324 (b) ©Davis Osborn/Alamy; 324–325 (bgd) ©Elmtree Images/ Alamy; 334 (l) ©Royalty-Free/Corbis; 334 bl ©Mitch Hrdlicka/Getty Images; 334 (b) ©photocuisine/Corbis; 334 (tl) ©John Kaprielian/Photo Researchers, Inc.; 334 (cl) ©Felicia Martinez/PhotoEdit; 334 (cl) ©Dorling Kindersley; 335 (t) ©David Murray/Dorling Kindersley; 334–335 (b) ©Maximilian Stock Ltd./FoodPix/Jupiter Images/Getty Images; 334–335 (c) ©Bischof/StockFood Munich/Stockfood America; 335 (bl) ©Teubner/Getty Images; 335 (bc) ©Dinodia Photo Library/FoodPix/Jupiter Images/Getty Images; 335 (tr) ©Eric Fowke/PhotoEdit; 336 (cl) ©Corbis; 336 (tr) © Estate of Yousuf Karsh/Julie Grahame/Camera Press/Retna; 336–337 (bgd) ©Taylor S. Kennedy/Getty Images; 338–339 (b) © Andrea Altemueller/Stock4B; 338–339 (t) ©Darwin Wiggett/Getty Images; 339 (b) ©Corbis; 340 (bgd) ©Andrea Altemueller/ Stock4B; 340 (r) ©Corbis; 341 ©Werner Forman/Art Resources, New York; 342 (bl) ©Royatly-Free/Corbis; 342 (t) ©Robin Macdougall/Getty Images; 342 (b) ©John Madama; 343 (r) ©PhotoDisc/Getty Images; 347 ©Jennifer Thermes/Getty Images; 354–355 (bgd) ©PhotoDisc/ Getty Images; 355 ©Brand X Images/Getty Images; 356–357 ©Houghton Mifflin Harcourt; 360–361 (bgd) ©PhotoDisc/Getty Images; 360 (tl) ©PhotoDisc/Getty Images; 360 (tl) ©PhotoDisc/Getty Images; 360 (b) ©Eyewire/Getty Images; 365 ©Dave King/Getty Images; 368 (tc) ©Royalty-Free/Corbis; 368 (tl) ©Peter Weimann/Animals Animals/Earth Sce 369 ©Toni Angermayer/Photo Researchers, Inc.; 370 (t) Conservation International/AP/Wide World Photos; 370 (b) ©DesignPics/Index Open; 370 (bgd) ©PhotoDisc/Getty Images; 371 (t Eraldo Peres/AP/Wide World Photos; 377 ©Natphotos/Getty Images; 378 (fungus) ©Jacques Jangoux/Visuals Unlimited, Inc.; 378 (ferns) ©Houghton Mifflin Harcourt; 378 (omnivore) ©Tom McHugh/Photo Researchers, Inc.; 378 (carnivore) ©John Giustina/Getty Images; 378 (herbivore) ©C. Allan Morgan/Peter Arnold, Inc.; 378 (sun) ©Getty Images; 378 (t) ©Ron Sanford/Corbis; 379 (b) ©Stuart Westmorland/Getty Images; 380 (t) ©Coleman/Alamy; 380 (b) ©Matt Jones/Alamy; 381 (t) ©Gavriel Jecan/Getty Images; 381 (b) ©James Balog/Getty Images; 382 (b) ©Royalty-Free/Corbis; 382 (t) ©Rick Sc hafer/Index Stock/Photolibrary; 38 (t) ©James P Blair/Getty Images; 383 (b) ©Craig Tuttle/Corbis; 384 (t) ©Digital Vision/Getty images; 384 (b) ©Janalee P. Caldwell and Laurie J. Vitt; 385 (b) ©Medio Images/Getty Imag 385 (br) ©Royalty-Free/Corbis; 385 (r) ©Tom & Pat Leeson/Photo Researchers, Inc.; 386 (t) ©Stockdisc/Getty Images; 387 (bl) ©Janalee P. Caldwell and Laurie J. Vitt; 387 (bgd) ©Digit Vision/Getty Images; 387 (br) ©Comstock; 388 (t) ©PhotoDisc/Getty Images; 388 (r) ©Digit Vision/Getty Images; 388 (bl) ©Janalee P. Caldwell and Laurie J. Vitt; 389 ©Fabio Colombin Medeiros/Animals Animals/Earth Scenes; 390–391 (bgd) ©Philip Coblentz/Brand X Pictures, Getty Images; 391 ©Rubberball/Alamy Images; 392 (bl) ©Corbis; 392 (br) ©Houghton Miffl Harcourt; 393 ©Houghton Mifflin Harcourt; 394 (t) ©PhotoDisc/Getty Images; 394–395 (bg ©PhotoDisc/Getty Images; 394 (b) ©Sue Cunningham Photography/Alamy; 398 ©M.Gunthe BIOS/Peter Arnold, Inc.; 399 ©PhotoDisc/Getty Images; 402–403 ©David Muench/Corbis; (b) ©Zigmund Leszczynski/Animals Animals/Earth Scenes; 404 (t) ©Renee Lynn/Corbis; 40 ©George Holton/Photo Researchers, Inc.; 404 ©Connie Bransilver/Photo Researchers, Inc.; ©K. Imamura/zefa/Corbis; 407 ©Billy Hustace/Getty Images; 408 (tr) ©Jacques Jangoux/Ph Researchers, Inc.; 408–409 (bgd) ©Gregory G. Dimijian, M.D./Photo Researchers, Inc.; 408 (b) ©Sue Cunningham Photography/Alamy; 410 (b) ©Jose Caldas/Brazilphotos; 410 (t) ©Jef Lepore/Photo Researchers, Inc.; 411 ©Frans Lanting/www.lanting.com/Minden Pictures; 41 ©Blend Images/Getty Images; 414–415 ©Frans Lemmens/Getty Images; 416 (br) ©Blickwin Alamy; 416 (t) ©Douglas Johns/Getty Images; 416 (bl) ©E. Braverman/Getty Images; 417 © Cole/Photodisc Green/Getty Images; 423 ©PhotoDisc/Getty Images; 424–425 ©Exactostock Superstock; 424 ©Superstock; 425 ©Houghton Mifflin Harcourt; 426 (bl) ©PhotoDisc/Getty Images; 426 (c) ©Houghton Mifflin Harcourt; 426 (br) ©PhotoDisc/Getty Images; 427 ©Houghton Mifflin Harcourt; 428–429 Market Day at Hojbro Plads, Copenhagen by Paul F ©Christie's Images/Corbis; 430 (t) ©PhotoDisc/Getty Images; 430 (b) ©PhotoDisc/Getty Im 430–431 (bgd) ©PhotoDisc/Getty Images; 434 (tl) ©Sarah Hadley/Alamy; 434 (tr) ©Dmitri Kessel/Time & Life Pictures/Getty Images; 434–435 (cr) ©Hitoshi Nishimura/Taxi Japan/Ge Images; 434 (cl) ©Fréderic Meylan/Sygma/Corbis; 434 (bl) ©Alamy; 434 (t bgd) ©Taxi/Get Images; 434 (bc) ©Hitoshi Nishimura/Taxi Japan/Getty Images; 435 ©Stockbyte/ Getty Im 434–435 (br) ©Eric Glenn/DK Stock/Getty Images; 438 (b) ©D. Hurst / Alamy; 439 ©Taxi Anderson/Getty Images; 449 (b) ©The Hoberman Collection/Alamy; 449 (t) ©The Hoberm Collection/Alamy; 452 (b) ©Royalty-Free/Corbis; 452 (t) ©Rosemary Calvert/Photographer Choice/Getty Images; 452 ©John W Banagan/Photographer's Choice/Getty Images; 454 (t) ©Eye Candy Images/Alamy; 454–455 (b) ©Jeff Mikkelson/Rubberball/Getty Images; 455 (t) ©Foodcollection/ Getty Images; 456 (b) ©Bildagentur-online.com/th-foto/Alamy; 456–457 (t) ©PhotoDisc/C Squared Studios/Getty Images; 457 (b) ©Alamy; 458 (b) ©numb/Alamy; 458 (t) ©Mike Surowiak/Stone/Getty Images; 459 (t) ©PhotoDisc Blue/Getty Images; 459 (©PhotoDisc Green/C Squared Studios/Getty Images; 460–461 (bgd) ©amana images inc./ Images; 460 (cl) ©Digital Vision/Alamy; 460 (bc) ©Houghton Mifflin Harcourt; 461 ©Hou Mifflin Harcourt; 462 (bl) ©PhotoDisc/Getty Images; 462 (bc) ©Artville/Getty Images; 463 ©Artville/Getty Images; 463 (br) ©Odilon Dimier/PhotoAlto/Age Fotostock America, Inc.; (t) ©Royalty-Free/Corbis; 464 (b) ©Royalty-Free/Corbis; 464–465 (bgd) ©PhotoDisc/Getty Images; 465 (b) ©Burke/Triolo Productions/FoodPix/Jupiter Images/Getty Images; 468 ©K Gregory & Wristies®; 472–473 (t) ©PhotoDisc/Getty Images; 472–473 (b) ©Corbis; 474 (r) ©Greg Stott/Masterfile; 474 (l) ©Greg Stott/Masterfile; 474 (bgd) ©David Noton Photogra Alamy; 475 (r) ©Wolfgang Kaehler/Corbis; 476 (r) ©Envision/Corbis; 476 (l) ©Burke/Triolo Productions/FoodPix /Jupiter Images/Getty Images; 477 ©Judith Collins/Alamy; 479 (b) © Threlfall/Alamy; 480 ©Iconica/Jade Albert/Getty Images; 481 (b) ©PhotoDisc/Getty Image (b inset) ©Corbis; 482 ©Corbis; 486 (c) ©Masterfile; 486 (t) ©PhotoDisc/Getty Images; 4 ©PhotoDisc/Getty Images; 486 (b) ©Tobbe/zefa/Corbis; 486 (b) ©PhotoDisc/Getty Image ©PhotoDisc/Getty Images; 494–495 (bgd) ©David R. Frazier/Photolibrary, Inc/Alamy Imag 494 ©Houghton Mifflin Harcourt; 495 ©Martin Sundberg/Corbis; 496–497 (all images) ©Houghton Mifflin Harcourt; 498–499 Glass Windows, Bahamas by Winslow Homer ©Brc Museum/Corbis; 500 (b) ©PhotoDisc/Getty Images; 500 (t) ©Judith River Dinosaur Institu 500–501 (bgd) ©Craig Lovell/Corbis; 504 (l) ©DK Limited/Corbis; 504–505 ©Peter Scoon Getty Images; 505 (b) ©Peter Scoones/Photo Researchers, Inc.; 508 (t) ©The Field Museu Sculpture by Brian Cooley. www.fieldmuseum.org (negative # GEO86197c).; 508–509 (bg ©Craig Lovell/Corbis; 518 (c) ©Mary Evans Picture Library/The Image Works; 518 (b) ©M Evans Picture Library/The Image Works; 518 (t) ©Tom McHugh/Photo Researchers, Inc.; ©Tom McHugh/Photo Researchers, Inc.; 520 (t) ©Francois Gohier/Photo Researchers, Inc. 520–521 (b) ©Melba Photo Agency/Alamy; 520–521 (bgd) ©Ernst Haas/Stone/Getty Imag 520–521 (t) ©A.J. Copley/Visuals Unlimited, Inc.; 521 (r) ©Louie Psihoyos/Corbis; 522 (b) ©Stockbyte/Getty Images; 522 (c) ©Davies & Starr/Getty Images; 522 (t) ©Colin Keates/ Images; 523 ©Pascal Goetgheluck/Photo Researchers, Inc.; 524 (b) ©Judith River Dinosa Institute; 525 (t) ©J. Woodcock/Judith River Dinosaur Institute; 526 ©/M. Murphy/Judit Dinosaur Institute; 527 ©J. Woodcock/Judith River Dinosaur Institute; 528 ©Judith River Dinosaur Institute; 529 ©/R. Martin/Judith River Dinosaur Institute; 530–531 (bgd) ©Jam Blair/Stockbyte/Getty Images; 530 ©Peter Casolino/Alamy Images; 531 ©JUPITERIMAGES/ Images; 532 (bl) ©Houghton Mifflin Harcourt; 532 (bc) ©C Squared Studios/Photodisc/G Images; 532 (br) ©Artville/Getty Images; 533 ©Houghton Mifflin Harcourt; 534 (b) ©Weatherstock; 534 (t) ©Corbis; 534–535 (bgd) ©PhotoDisc/Getty Images; 538 (b) ©Phc Getty Images; 538–539 (bgd) ©Pixtal/SuperStock; 539 (t) ©Getty Images; 539 (b) ©Darr Gulin/Corbis; 542 (l) ©David J. & Janice L. Frent Collection/Corbis; 542 (r) ©Corbis; 542 (bgd) ©Cliff Farlinger/Alamy Images; 543 (t) National Park Service; 545 (b) ©Royalty-Fre Corbis; 545 (t) ©Daniel Aguilar/Reuters/Corbis; 546 (l) ©Patrickcone Photography; 546– (bgd) ©Ray Mathis/EcoStock; 547–550 (paintings) ©Thomas Hallstein/outsight.com; 548 (paintings) ©Chuck Mitchell; 549 (b) ©Brad Mitchell/Mira; 550 (b) ©Tom Till; 551 ©Patri Photography; 552 (t) AP/Wide World Photos; 552 (b) AP/Wide World Photos; 553 ©Digita Vision/ Getty Images; 554 (t) Photo courtesy of the U. S. Geological Survey; 554 (b) Phc courtesy of the U. S. Geological Survey; 554–555 (bgd) ©Reuters/Corbis; 555 (c) Photo of the U. S. Geological Survey; 555 (b) Photo courtesy of the U. S. Geological Survey; 5 Photo courtesy of the U. S. Geological Survey; 556 (b) ©Bettmann/Corbis; 556 (bgd) ©C 556 (r) ©Getty Images; 556 (l) ©Jane Sapinsky/SuperStock; 557 (b) ©Terry W. Eggers/Cc 557 (t) ©Heinrich Van Den Berg/Gallo Images/Getty Images; 564–565 (bgd) ©Susan Got Alamy; 564 ©Dave Bunnell; 565 ©Dave Bunnell; 566 ©Photodisc/Getty Images; 567 ©H Mifflin Harcourt.